Robert Schumann, Carl Czerny, Horatio Richmond Palmer

Palmer's Piano Primer

Robert Schumann, Carl Czerny, Horatio Richmond Palmer

Palmer's Piano Primer

ISBN/EAN: 9783337371388

Printed in Europe, USA, Canada, Australia, Japan

Cover: Foto ©Thomas Meinert / pixelio.de

More available books at **www.hansebooks.com**

PALMER'S
PIANO PRIMER:

A SYSTEMATIC AND CLEAR EXPLANATION OF THE FUNDAMENTAL PRINCIPLES OF

PIANO-FORTE PLAYING.

Designed for the assistance of Teachers, and as a Text-book for Classes or private Pupils

Containing

A Scientific Exposition of the Rudiments of Musical Notation and Piano-Forte *Technique*, illlustrated by more than 400 examples with 168 explanatory notes,

TOGETHER WITH

A List embracing more than 200 TECHNICAL STUDIES, SONATAS, etc., graded, from those for beginners up to the MOST ELABORATE WORKS OF THE VARIOUS WRITERS FOR THE PIANO-FORTE ;

TO WHICH IS ADDED

"SCHUMANN'S 68 RULES FOR BEGINNERS;" "CZERNY'S LETTERS ON THE ART OF PLAYING THE PIANO-FORTE;" "BURROW'S GUIDE TO PRACTICE;" AND A "PRONOUNCING DICTIONARY" OF MORE THAN 300 MUSICAL TERMS;

THE WHOLE FORMING A MUSICAL

VADE MECUM.

BY

H. R. PALMER, MUS. DOC.,

AUTHOR OF

"PALMER'S THEORY OF MUSIC," ETC

PUBLISHED BY H. R. PALMER.

LOCK-BOX, 2841,

NEW YORK.

PREFACE.

THIS PRIMER is intended as a text-book, a *multum in parvo*, containing the gist of the whole matter, which is to be elaborated by the teacher according to the necessities of the case.

It is recommended that the pupils be required to commit the questions and answers to memory, (a few at each lesson, 5 to 20, according to the capacity for memorizing,) and recite them at the beginning of the next lesson; this would, in the course of six or twelve months, place much important information at the pupil's disposal, thereby saving the teacher's valuable time for those things which cannot be learned from books, while the learners would stand on a broader foundation of musical knowledge, with no perceptible interference with the time of lessons; in fact, it would in the end save their time, for, with increased knowledge, they will be able to comprehend the explanations and elucidations of the teacher much more rapidly, thereby insuring greater advancement in the same length of time.

Parents, or even the older children of the family can, with the aid of this work, see that a thorough foundation is laid in the minds of beginners, and thus accomplish a great saving, for what is thus learned will save the teacher's time by just so much.

If the teacher thinks best, the Chapter on the Key-Board may be committed to memory first.

The plans of fingering the scales, and intervals, should also be committed to memory, and applied in all other cases. They are intended to be used as we use Webster's Dictionary—when in doubt as to a certain way of fingering, turn to the PRIMER; and while it is not intended as a book of practice, still the exhaustive treatment of the scales will render the PRIMER useful as a practice-book, *so far as they are concerned.* An elastic cord stretched across the book-rack will serve to keep the book open.

While the author has not hesitated to take good ideas from whatever source he could find them, he is greatly indebted to Dr. WM. MASON and his associate editor, Mr. W. S. B. MATHEWS (and to Messrs. OLIVER DITSON & CO., publishers of *Mason's Piano-forte Technics*), for many important principles not found elsewhere.

Among the many sources from which the author has gleaned, he takes pleasure in acknowledging the admirable works of Mr. LOUIS PLAIDY, Professor of the Piano-forte in the Conservatorium of Leipzig; Mr. ALOYS BIDEZ, LL.D., from the National Conservatoire at Brussels, and Mr. ERNEST PAUER, Professor of the Piano-forte in the National Training School in London. His acknowledgments are also due, and are hereby extended to the many other gentlemen of known ability, whose hearty support and sympathy have been of great value, and whose letters of commendation are printed herewith.

Especially is he under obligation to Mr. W. H. SHERWOOD of Boston, Mr. A. R. PARSONS and Mr. CARYL FLORIO of New York, who have read the work in MS., and who have enriched its pages by the addition of such notes as have been suggested by their large experience. These notes are signed by the initials of the writers.

H. R. PALMER.

NEW YORK, January 15, 1885.

What Prominent Musicians say of the Primer.

DR. H. R. PALMER:

DEAR SIR:—It gives me pleasure to be able to confidently recommend your "PIANO PRIMER." Although small in size it is comprehensive, and contains the pith of the subject matter of which it treats, expressed in clear and concise language. As a text-book it will be very useful and valuable to students of music, as well as to others who desire practical information concerning the main and essential points of Piano-forte playing.

Yours sincerely,

ORANGE, N. J., May 6th, 1885.   WILLIAM MASON.

DR. H. R. PALMER:

MY DEAR SIR:—This is an age of progress, even in works of instruction for Piano students, where I have sometimes believed people were never going to change for the better! We need new life, new rules, and intelligence in the methods for elementary instruction, if we would raise the standard of Piano-playing to something more artistic, and make that beautiful instrument a source of real enjoyment.

I am very glad to see the evidence of sound knowledge, of clear and concise diction, modern improvement and valuable contents in your new work. The information it contains is just that which is needed for intelligent Piano students, and it is so arranged as to prove of unmistakable value as a reliable book of reference for both beginners and advanced musicians. I feel highly honored that you should, among so many able authorities, give my humble efforts a place therein.

Wishing the work the eminent success it deserves, and the musical public the full benefit thereof, I remain,

Most respectfully yours,

BOSTON, MASS., Sept. 24th, 1884.   WM. H. SHERWOOD.

MY DEAR DR. PALMER:

Your intelligent and indefatigable industry in research, accumulation, systematization and classification, has produced in your new "PIANO PRIMER" a most meaty volume, which, by comparison, reduces at once to insignificance every previous work of the kind.

The mastery of its clearly worded and richly abundant contents, ample illustrations and ingenious tables and diagrams, will afford the student an adequate foundation for the most ambitious superstructure of musical knowledge; while simply for the purpose of reference it is one of the very most useful hand-books the Piano-forte teacher can put into the hands of earnest and intelligent pupils.

Pray accept my sincere and friendly congratulations in advance upon the certain and great success awaiting this your newest work.

Very truly yours,

N. Y., Feb. 27th, 1885.   ALBERT R. PARSONS.

HERSHEY SCHOOL OF MUSICAL ART.

DR. H. R. PALMER:

MY DEAR SIR:—I congratulate you upon the treasures of pianistic information, which you have gathered into your "PIANO PRIMER." It is just such a text-book as I have long wanted to use, and I shall take great pleasure in recommending it to every pupil in our School.

The work embodies a vast amount of important technical material, while the addition of copious notes by our most eminent authorities on the subject of Piano-forte playing renders the book of untold value.

You are entitled to hearty thanks from every music teacher, for providing a manual so concise and comprehensive, which, if used with intelligence, will greatly facilitate his labors.

Yours very truly,

CHICAGO, Sept. 15th, 1885.   CLARENCE EDDY.

DR. H. R. PALMER:

DEAR SIR:—The most cursory examination of your PIANO PRIMER must reveal the extreme value of its contents, while a more careful study of the work should most certainly compel the unqualified admiration of any person interested in a systematic, clear and scientific presentation of the fundamental principles of musical art.

Any student of the Piano who does not acquaint himself with this work, loses thereby a valuable assistant to intelligent practice, and it is not too much to say that ignorance of its contents on the part of the professional musician implies a lack of interest in musical literature far from encouraging. Trusting that the work will be recognized as a most essential factor in the student's development, and assuring you of my hearty endorsement of the same, I am

Very sincerely,   ALBERT A. STANLEY.

PROVIDENCE, R. I., Dec. 30th, 1885.

THE PETERSILEA ACADEMY OF MUSIC, ELOCUTION AND LANGUAGES.

MY DEAR DR. PALMER:

Having carefully examined "PALMER'S PIANO PRIMER," before going to press, I can conscientiously say that it is far in advance of any similar book of its kind in existence, and ought to be used in connection with the best system of Piano instruction. I shall take great pleasure in using it as a text-book in this school, and placing it in the hands of all our pupils, whether instrumental or vocal.

CARLYLE PETERSILEA.

BOSTON, MASS., Sept. 1st, 1884.

DR. H. R. PALMER:

MY DEAR SIR:—I have carefully examined your PIANO FORTE PRIMER, and take pleasure in expressing my commendation of the work. It is clear, accurate and concise, and much superior to all works of the sort previously published.   Yours very truly,

S. N. PENFIELD.

NEW YORK, Dec. 24th, 1885.

DR. H. R. PALMER:

DEAR SIR:—I have examined somewhat carefully your PIANO PRIMER, and find that it embodies all that is desirable in such a book. It is without doubt the most perfect work of the kind ever published.

There has been two noticeable imperfections in all Piano Primers namely: the conciseness of definition with brief treatment of subjects, and their inadaptability to Piano instruction. These defects you have completely overcome in your work, besides giving a fair recognition of the numerous improvements made in modern mode of instruction of the Piano-Forte. The work has not only my unqualified personal endorsement, but I shall lose no opportunity in extending its usefulness and popularity

Very respectfully yours,   THEO. PRESSER.

PHILADELPHIA, PA., Dec. 28th, 1885.

" With rare insight, you have perceived the universal needs of musical students, and have supplied them with a *vade mecum*, marvellously well selected, perfectly arranged, clearly and definitely stated. Such works have only to appear, and to gain a reading, in order to be recognized ever afterward as indispensable."—*L. H. Sherwood, N. Y.*

" After careful perusal I am happy to say that it is a very valuable acquisition to students and teachers. I shall certainly use it for my pupils and urge them to make a careful study of every detail which you have so clearly and ably explained."—*Calixa Lavallee, Mass.*

" Cannot fail to bring about most rapid and tangible results. 'Tis certainly '*multum in parvo.*' It surpasses *everything of the kind* I have seen, either in this country or in Europe, and should be in the hands of every student."—*L. W. Wheeler, Mass.*

" I don't remember when I have examined a book that I can recommend with so much enthusiasm. There is no doubt of its becoming a standard text-book in all our musical schools."—*M. L. Bartlett, Ills.*

" The book as a whole is so comprehensive that I think I shall do the same that Mr. EDDY yesterday told me he would, viz., recommend, or require, pupils to get it."—*W. S. B. Mathews, Ills.*

"Your PIANO PRIMER is miles better than any other student book I have seen. The music student who has not a copy has my profound commiseration."—*Eugene Thayer, New York City.*

" Even a cursory investigation shows that it will meet a want. Often receive enquiries for just such a book. Shall be glad to introduce it in my work."—*Emil Liebling, Ills.*

" A text-book whose value will be appreciated by all music teachers who wish to save themselves the trouble of endless oral explanations."—*Chicago Tribune.*

"I have read your PRIMER with great interest. It is by far the most complete and valuable work of its kind I have seen.—*E. S. Hoadley, Mass.*

" An excellent work; am using it in my Conservatory of Music; shall recommend it to all my teachers and pupils,"—*Johannes Goetze, Mo.*

" Am greatly pleased with the PRIMER. A small name for so comprehensive a work."—*M. M. Macdonald, M. D., N. Y.*

" A really excellent work, which deserves the attention of all Pianoforte teachers and pupils."—*Karl Merz, Ohio.*

"There is more knowledge to be gleaned from one page than from five of many other works."—*M. Owen, N. C.*

" It must prove of great assistance to the earnest teacher, and invaluable to the pupil."—*F. O. Jones, N. Y.*

"Like your *Theory of Music*, your PIANO PRIMER will be my steady companion."—*H. A. Kelso, Jr., Ills.*

"Consider it the best and most complete of any yet issued. Shall recommend it."—*G. C. Smith, Ills.*

"So nicely, too, is it printed and bound, that in *body* as well as *soul* it is a gem."—*M. A. Nelson, Mass.*

"I am much pleased with the book, and shall use it with all my pupils."—*M. H. Burnham. Vt.*

"Just what is needed on every Piano. I shall introduce it among my pupils."—*Albert Hook, Wis.*

" It is the best and most comprehensive work I have ever seen."—*S. C. Davis, Baltimore, Md.*

" It stands alone, so far is it ahead of its predecessors."—*Aloys Bidez, LL. D., N. C.*

" Will benefit any Piano pupil, and equally so any Piano teacher."—*S. M. King, O.*

"Excels everything of the kind I have ever examined."–*R. R. Ebright, Ind.*

" A most valuable addition to my musical library."—*M. Stillwell, Ills.*

"This will be just the thing, I think."—*A. M. Johnson, Mass.*

" Consider it a work of great value."—*E. H. Plowe, Ills.*

PALMER'S PIANO PRIMER.

CHAPTER I.
TONES AND THEIR REPRESENTATIONS.

LENGTH.

1. *What is* SOUND?
Sound is anything audible.

2. *What is a* TONE?
A tone is a sound in which pitch is perceptible.

3. *How many properties has a tone, and what are they called?*
Three. Length, Pitch, and Power.

4. *What is the meaning of "length" as applied to a tone?*
The Length of a tone is its property of continuance, or duration.

5. *How is the length of tones represented?*
By characters called NOTES.

6. *How many different kinds of notes are there in general use, and what are their names?*
Eight. The double-whole note; the whole note; the half note; the quarter note; the eighth note; the sixteenth note; the thirty-second note; and the sixty-fourth note.

7. *Why are these names given to notes?*
Because of their relative lengths: A half note is so called because it represents one-half the duration of a whole note; a quarter note represents one quarter of the duration of a whole note; an eighth note represents one eighth of the duration of a whole note; a sixteenth note represents one sixteenth of the duration of a whole note; a thirty-second note represents one thirty-second of the duration of a whole note; and a sixty-fourth note represents one sixty-fourth of the duration of a whole note.

NOTE 1.—The Double-whole note (‖𝄎‖) or (‖𝄎‖) representing a tone double the length of a whole note will be frequently found in Church music.

8. *How is the whole note made?*
Like the letter O, elongated (𝅝)

9. *How is the half note made?*
With an open head and a stem (𝅗𝅥)

10. *How is the quarter note made?*
With a full head and a stem (𝅘𝅥)

11. *How is the eighth note made?*
With a full head, a stem and a hook (𝅘𝅥𝅮)

7

Ex. 1.

TABLE OF NOTES

TECHNICAL NAMES				NOTES.	TECHNICAL NAMES		
German.					*American.*	*English.*	*French.*
Die Ganze.				o	Whole note.	Semibreve.	Ronde.
Die Halbe.				2	Half note.	Minim.	Blanche.
Das Viertel.				4	Quarter note.	Crotchet.	Noire.
Das Achtel.				8	Eighth note.	Quaver.	Croche.
Das Sechszehntel.				16	Sixteenth note.	Semiquaver.	Double croche.
Das Zweiundreissigstel.				32	Thirty-second note.	Demisemiquaver.	Triple croche.

NOTE 2.—It is not thought best to include the double-whole note, the sixty-fourth note and the hundred-and-twenty-eighth note here, as they would require the enlarging of the table beyond convenient limits.

12. *How is the sixteenth note made ?*

With a full head, a stem and two hooks (♬)

13. *How is the thirty-second note made ?*

With a full head, a stem and three hooks (♬)

14. *How is the sixty-fourth note made ?*

With a full head, a stem and four hooks (♬)

15. *Have notes an absolute value as regards length ?*

They have not. Their value is entirely relative. **In a lively** piece the notes are much shorter than in a slow piece.

RESTS.

16. *What are* RESTS ?

Rests are characters indicating suspension of tone.

17. *How many kinds of rests are there, and what are their names ?*

Seven. The whole rest; the half rest; the quarter rest; the eighth rest; the sixteenth rest; the thirty-second rest; and the sixty-fourth rest

NOTE 3.—See Note 5 for double-whole rest.

18. *How is the whole rest made ?*

A square block below a line (━)

19. *How is the half rest made ?*

A square block above a line (▬)

20. *How is the quarter rest made ?*

Like the figure 7 reversed (𝄽)

NOTE 4.—During the past few years a different style of quarter rest has been introduced, thus (𝄽) or 𝄽, which is less likely to be confounded with the eighth rest.

21. *How is the eighth rest made ?*

Like the figure 7 (𝄾)

22. *How is the sixteenth rest made ?*

Like the figure 7 with two-heads (𝄿)

23. *How is the thirty-second rest made ?*

Like the figure 7 with three heads (𝅀)

24. *How is the sixty-fourth rest made ?*

Like the figure 7 with four heads (𝅁)

25. *As regards length, rests correspond to what ?*

To the notes of the same denomination.

EX. 2. RESTS WITH THEIR CORRESPONDING NOTES.

Whole note and rest.	Half note and rest.	Quarter note and rest.	Eighth note and rest.	Sixteenth note and rest.	Thirty-second note and rest.
○ ▬	♩ ▬	♩ 𝄽	♪ 𝄾	♬ 𝄿	♬ 𝅀

NOTE 5.—Sometimes the whole rest is used as a whole measure rest; when so used, it fills the measure. Frequently a rest of two, three or more measures is required, in which case it is expressed by a heavy stroke or strokes over which is written the number of measures included in the rest, thus:—

EX. 3.

CHAPTER II.

TONES AND THEIR REPRESENTATIONS.—Continued.

PITCH.

26. *What is* PITCH ?

Pitch is a property of highness or lowness, without some degree of which, no tone can exist.

NOTE 6.—The terms "high and low," as applied to tones, require some explanation. A tone which is the result of very rapid vibrations, is called a "high" tone. And a tone which is the result of very slow vibrations, is called a "low" tone. "High" and "low" when so used must be considered as TECHNICAL TERMS, for in no other sense can one tone be said to be HIGHER than another; in other words, tones, as such, have no altitude.

27. *How are the pitches of tones named ?*

By the names of the first seven letters of the alphabet, A, B, C, D, E, F, and G.

28. *How, and from what are the pitches of tones reckoned?*

Upward and downward from the pitch called MIDDLE C.

29. *Why is the pitch Middle C so called ?*

Because it is midway between the extreme high tones and the extreme low tones.

30. *In ascending, what order is observed in naming the pitches?*

The alphabetical order; the pitch above A is B, then C, D, E, F, G, etc.

31. *If we wish to go above G, how do we proceed?*

The pitch above G is A, then B, C, D, etc., repeating as frequently as is necessary.

32. *In descending, how are the pitches named ?*

Backward; G, F, E, D, C, B, A, etc.

33. *If we wish to go below A, how do we proceed?*

The pitch below A is G, then F, E, D, C, B, A, G, F, etc., repeating as often as is necessary.

34. *How are the pitches of tones represented ?*

By a character called a STAFF.

35. *Of what does the staff consist?*

It consists mainly of five parallel lines and the spaces which belong to them; and is frequently enlarged by means of short added lines and spaces, above and below.

Ex. 4. Staff with Added Lines and Spaces.

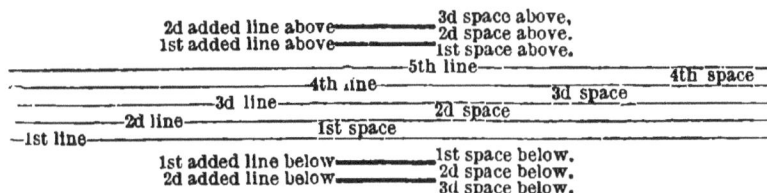

```
                                           3d space above,
  2d added line above                      2d space above.
  1st added line above                     1st space above.
                             5th line
                       4th line                         4th space
                3d line                      3d space
         2d line                   2d space
  1st line                1st space
  1st added line below                      1st space below.
  2d added line below                       2d space below.
                                            3d space below.
```

36. *What is each line and space of the staff called?*
A degree.

37. *How are the degrees of the staff numbered?*
Upward from the lowest of the long lines.

38. *How many different kinds of staffs are there in general use, and what are they called?*
Two.   The Treble staff and Bass staff.

39. *How are these two staffs distinguished?*
By characters called CLEFS.

40. *What clef always accompanies the Treble staff?*
The Treble clef (𝄞).

41. *What clef always accompanies the Bass staff?*
The Bass clef (𝄢) or (𝄢).

42. *Are staffs generally used singly, or are they usually combined?*
In Piano music they are always combined by means of a character called a BRACE { or ‖.

Ex. 5. Staffs with Clefs, combined by a Brace

43. *Which degree of the Treble staff represents Middle C?*
The first added line below.

Ex. 6. The Middle C.

Middle C.

44. *Name the order of pitch representations on the Treble staff from Middle C upward.*

The added line below represents Middle C; the space below represents D; the first line E; the first space F; the second line G; the second space A; the third line B; the third space C; the fourth line D; the fourth space E; the fifth line F; the space above G; etc.

Ex. 7.   Pitch Representations of the Treble Staff.

45. *Which degree of the Bass staff represents Middle C?*
The first added line above.

Ex. 8.   Middle C.

46. *Name the order of pitch representations on the Bass staff from Middle C downward.*

The added line above represents Middle C; the space above represents B; the fifth line A; the fourth space G; the fourth line F; the third space E; the third line D; the second space C; the second line B; the first space A; the first line G; the space below F; etc.

Ex. 9.   Pitch Representations of the Bass Staff.

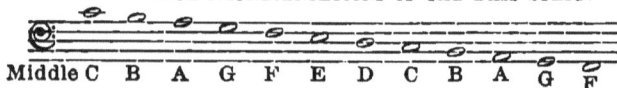

Ex. 10.   Pitch Representations of Treble and Bass Staffs.

CHAPTER III.

MEASURES, BARS, ACCENTS, AND TIME SIGNATURES.

47. *What are* BARS, *and for what are they used?*
Bars are small lines drawn perpendicularly across the staff, to indicate the beginning, or strong pulse of the measure.

48 *What is a* MEASURE?
A measure is a group of two or more regularly recurring pulsations.

49. *How is a measure represented?*
A measure is represented by a portion of the staff between two bars.

EX. 11. MEASURES AND BARS.

Bar.   Bar.   Bar.   Bar.

——Measure.—— ——Measure.—— ——Measure.——

50. *A measure having two pulsations is called what?*
Double measure.

51. *A measure having three pulsations is called what?*
Triple measure.

52. *A measure having four pulsations is called what?*
Quadruple measure.

53. *A measure having six pulsations is called what?*
Sextuple measure.

54. *A measure having nine pulsations is called what?*
Compound Triple measure.

55. *A measure having twelve pulsations is called what?*
Compound Quadruple measure.

56. *What is a Time Signature?*
It is the fraction which is always placed at the beginning of a composition.

57. *What does it signify?*
It has a two-fold signification; 1st, its upper figure tells what kind of measure is used, i. e., how many pulsations in each measure; and, 2d, its lower figure tells what kind of a note is reckoned to each pulse,

thus: $\frac{2}{4}$ indicates *double measure*, with a *quarter note* to each pulse, and is read, *two quarter notes (or their equivalent) will fill a measure.*

Ex. 12. $\frac{2}{4}$ MEASURES OF VARIOUS FORMS.

58. *Is a quarter note always reckoned to each pulse?*

Usually a quarter note is reckoned to each pulse; but the whole note, the half-note, the eighth-note, and even the sixteenth-note may be reckoned to a pulse, at the option of the composer.

59. *When the time signature is $\frac{2}{2}$ how is it read?*

Two half notes (or their equivalent) will fill a measure.

Ex. 13. $\frac{2}{2}$ MEASURES OF VARIOUS FORMS.

60. *When the time signature is $\frac{3}{2}$ how is it read?*
Three half notes (or their equivalent) will fill a measure.
61. *When the time signature is $\frac{3}{4}$ how is it read?*
Three quarter notes (or their equivalent) will fill a measure.
62. *When the time signature is $\frac{3}{8}$ how is it read?*
Three eighth notes (or their equivalent) will fill a measure.

Ex. 14. THE DIFFERENT KINDS OF TRIPLE MEASURE.

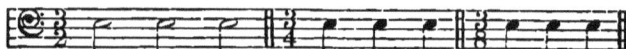

63. *When the time signature is $\frac{4}{2}$ how is it read?*
Four half notes (or their equivalent) will fill a measure.
64. *When the time signature is $\frac{4}{4}$ how is it read?*
Four quarter notes (or their equivalent) will fill a measure.
65. *When the time signature is $\frac{4}{8}$ how is it read?*
Four eighth notes (or their equivalent) will fill a measure.
66. *When the time signature is $\frac{4}{16}$ how is it read?*
Four sixteenth notes (or their equivalent) will fill a measure.

Ex. 15. THE DIFFERENT KINDS OF QUADRUPLE MEASURE.

67. *When the time signature is* $\frac{6}{4}$ *how is it read ?*
Six quarter notes (or their equivalent) will fill a measure.
68. *When the time signature is* $\frac{6}{8}$ *how is it read ?*
Six eighth notes (or their equivalent) will fill a measure.

Ex. 16.   The different kinds of Sextuple Measure.

69. *When the time signature is* $\frac{9}{4}$ *how is it read ?*
Nine quarter notes (or their equivalent) will fill a measure.
70. *When the time signature is* $\frac{9}{8}$ *how is it read ?*
Nine eighth notes (or their equivalent) will fill a measure.

Ex. 17.   The different kinds of Compound Triple Measure.

71. *When the time signature is* $\frac{12}{4}$ *how is it read ?*
Twelve quarter notes (or their equivalent) will fill a measure.
72. *When the time signature is* $\frac{12}{8}$ *how is it read ?*
Twelve eighth notes (or their equivalent) will fill a measure.

Ex. 18.   The different kinds of Compound Quardruple Measure.

73. *How is* $\frac{4}{4}$ *measure sometimes indicated ?*
By the letter C.
74. *How is* $\frac{2}{2}$ *measure sometimes indicated ?*
By a letter ₵ with a line drawn through it.
75. *What were such measures formerly called ?*
" Common Time."

Note 7.—The following table shows all the time signatures in common use.

Ex. 19.   The various time signatures.

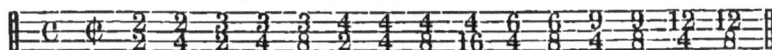

Note 8.—The former complicated classification of measures, such as Common; Half-Common; Simple; Common Compound; Simple Common, etc., is now being abandoned by our first class teachers as simply compounded nonsense. It is to be hoped that the old time-signatures C and ₵ will also soon become obsolete.

76. *What is accent?*

A slight stress upon a certain pulsation, to mark its position in the measure.

77. *Which pulse of double measure is accented?*

The first.

Ex. 20.   DOUBLE MEASURE.   First pulse accented.

78. *Which pulse of triple measure is accented?*

The first.

Ex. 21.   TRIPLE MEASURE.   First pulse accented.

79. *Which pulses of quadruple measure are accented?*

Quadruple measure has a primary accent on the first pulse, and a secondary accent on the third.

Ex. 22.   QUADRUPLE MEASURE.   First and third pulses accented.

80. *Which pulses of sextuple measure are accented?*

A primary accent on the first and a secondary accent on the fourth.

Ex. 23.   SEXTUPLE MEASURE.   First and fourth pulses accented.

81. *Which pulses of compound triple measure are accented?*

A primary accent on the first, and secondary accents on the fourth and seventh.

Ex. 24.   COMPOUND TRIPLE MEASURE.   First, fourth and seventh pulses accented.

82. *Which pulses of compound quadruple measure are accented?*

A primary accent on the first, and secondary accents on the fourth, seventh and tenth.

Ex. 25.   COMPOUND QUADRUPLE MEASURE.   First, fourth, seventh and tenth
pulses accented.

CHAPTER IV

THE DOT; THE REPEAT; BIS; D.C., Etc.

83. *What is the use of a dot?*

The dot has three uses:—1st, when placed after a note or rest; 2d, when placed under or over notes; and 3d, when placed in the spaces of the staff beside a bar.

84. *When placed after a note, what does it signify?*

It adds one-half to the time value of the note after which it is placed, thus:—

A dotted whole note, (𝅝.) equals a whole note and a half-note, ... (𝅝𝅗𝅥).

A dotted half-note, (𝅗𝅥.) equals a half-note and a quarter note, ... (𝅗𝅥𝅘𝅥).

A dotted quarter note, (𝅘𝅥.) equals a quarter note and an eighth note, . . (𝅘𝅥𝅘𝅥𝅮).

A dotted eighth note, (𝅘𝅥𝅮.) equals an eighth note and a sixteenth note, . . (𝅘𝅥𝅮𝅘𝅥𝅯).

A dotted sixteenth note, (𝅘𝅥𝅯.) equals a sixteenth note and a thirty-second note, (𝅘𝅥𝅯𝅘𝅥𝅰)·

85. *When placed after a rest, what does it indicate?*

As with notes, a dot adds one half to the time value of the rest after which it is placed, thus:—

A dotted whole rest, (𝄻·) equals a whole rest and a half rest, ... (𝄻 𝄼).

A dotted half rest, (𝄼·) equals a half rest and a quarter rest, ... (𝄼 𝄽).

A dotted quarter rest, (𝄽 ·) equals a quarter rest and an eighth rest, . . (𝄽 𝄾).

A dotted eighth rest, (𝄾 .) equals an eighth rest and a sixteenth rest, . . (𝄾 𝄿).

A dotted sixteenth rest, (𝄿 .) equals a sixteen th rest and a thirty-second rest, (𝄿 𝅀).

Ex. 26. THE TIME VALUE OF A DOT.

86. *What effect have double dots when placed after notes?*

Double dots add to the time value three-quarters of the length of the note which they follow; in other words, the first dot adds one-half and the second dot adds one-half as much as the first dot, thus:—

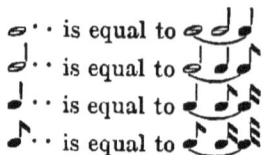

87. *When placed after rests, what does the double dot denote?*

As with double-dotted notes so with double-dotted rests, thus:—

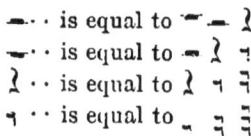

EX. 27. THE TIME VALUE OF DOUBLE DOTS.

88. *When dots are placed over or under notes, what do they signify?*

That the tones should be performed in a short and distinct manner, and only sustained one-half their usual length.

89. *When dots are thus employed, they are called what?*

Semi-staccato marks.

EX. 28. SEMI-STACCATO.

90. *When dots are placed in the spaces of the staff beside a bar, what do they signify?*

They indicate a repetition; if placed *before* the bar, the previous passage is to be performed twice in succession before proceeding to the next.

EX. 29. THE REPEAT.

91. *When dots are placed after a bar, what is their signification?*

When dots are placed *after* a bar, the performer should take particular notice of them, for he will soon be sent back to them by a set of dots *before* a bar further on, and the passage between the two sets of dots must be performed twice in succession before proceeding beyond.

Ex. 30. THE REPEAT. Continued.

etc.

92. *What is the meaning of 1st time and 2d time, which frequently accompany repeat marks?*

They denote that when the passage is repeated, the measure marked 1st time is to be omitted, and that which is marked 2d time performed instead.

Ex. 31. 1ST TIME AND 2D TIME.

NOTE 9.—The pupil will frequently meet with the words *Prima Volta* and *Seconda Volta* or their abbreviations, 1ma, 2da, instead of 1st time and 2d time.

93. *What is the meaning of Bis?*

It means twice, and signifies that the passage over which it is placed is to be performed twice in succession before proceeding beyond.

Ex. 32. BIS.

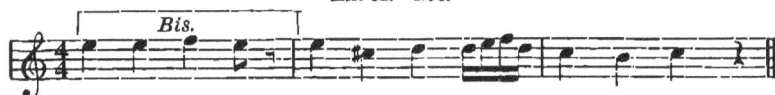

94. *What is the meaning of Da Capo,* or D. C.?*

Da, from the; *Capo,* commencement; which means repeat from the beginning.

NOTE 10.—The letters D.·C. and the words Da Capo, are an abbreviation of the Italian sentence "Da Capo al Fine," (pronounced dah-*cah*-po al *fee*-nay), which, freely translated, means *Da,* from the; *Capo,* head, or beginning; *al,* to the; *Fine,* end.

Ex. 33. DA CAPO.

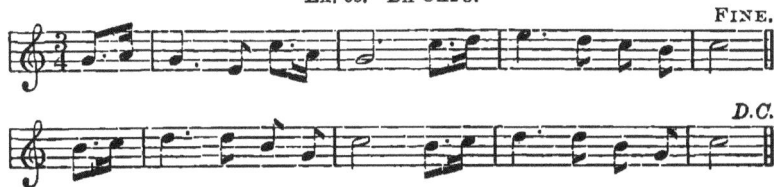

---

* Pronounced dah-*cah*-po.

95. *What is the meaning of D. S. ?*

D. S. is an abbreviation of the Italian words *Dal Segno*,* and means return to the sign ($:S:$).

Ex. 34.   DAL SEGNO.

96. *What is a phrase?*

A phrase is a series of designs, or motives, so joined as to have a well-determined motion and repose.

97. *How is a phrase indicated?*

Sometimes by a DOUBLE BAR;

Ex. 35   PHRASE-MARK.

sometimes by a long curved line called a *phrase-mark*, and sometimes by both.

NOTE 11.—Inasmuch as the curved line is already used, both as a *tie*, and a *slur*, and as both ties and slurs are frequently used in phrases, a different mark to indicate the phrase is much needed.   If all would unite in using the *bracket* (⌐‾‾‾‾¬) as a phrase mark, much confusion would thereby be avoided.

98. *What is a section, and how indicated?*

A section is a series of two or more phrases, sometimes called a strain.

99. *What is a period?*

A period is a series of four or more phrases, each having a well-defined motion and repose, so related to each other as to produce the impression of completeness.

100. *What is a hold, or pause, and what is its signification?*

The hold or pause consists of a short curved line and dot ($\frown$ or $\smile$), and denotes that the tone or rest thus indicated must be prolonged.

Ex. 36.   THE HOLD, OR PAUSE.

NOTE 12.—There is a tacit understanding, so far as instrumental music is concerned, that a note (or rest) with a hold over it receives about twice its normal time.   When more or less is absolutely desired, careful composers (as are most of the moderns) indicate the fact by adding to the hold the words *lunga* or *picolo*; sometimes even writing the full phrase *lunga pausa* (long pause), *picolo pausa* (little or short pause), in addition to the hold itself. C. F.

* Pronounced *Dahl Sayn'-yo.*

101. *What is the close, and for what is it used?*

The close consists of two double bars (over which a hold is sometimes placed), and denotes the end of a composition.

Ex. 37.   THE CLOSE.

NOTE 13.—The Italian word Fine (pronounced *fee*-nay) is frequently used to indicate the end of a composition.

102. *What is a TIE, and for what is it used?*

A tie consists of a curved line, and serves to connect two notes when they are written on the same degree of the staff. It indicates that the tone is to be prolonged the total length of the notes thus connected. (Enharmonic tones are frequently tied.)

Ex 38.   THE TIE.

103. *What is a slur?*

A slur is a curved line which connects two or more notes when written on different degrees of the staff, and indicates that the tones so connected are to be performed in a smooth and connected manner.

Ex. 39.   THE SLUR.

103½. *What does* STACCATO *mean, and how is it indicated?*

Staccato means that the tones should be performed in a short and distinct manner, and sustained only one-fourth as long as represented. It is indicated by points placed over or under the notes.

Ex. 39½.   STACCATO.

Written.   Performed.

REMARK. 1—As regards the answer to No. 100, Dr. Mason suggests that it would be better to call this sign ⌢ a HOLD when placed over or under a *note*, and a PAUSE when placed over or under a *rest*.

CHAPTER V.

INTERMEDIATE TONES, INTERVALS, Etc.

104. *What are intermediate tones?*

Those tones which occur between the regular tones of a key.

105. *How are intermediate tones represented?*

By the aid of characters called sharps (♯), flats (♭) and cancels (♮).*

106. *For what is a sharp (♯) used?*

To indicate an intermediate tone the tendency from which is upward.

107. *For what is a flat (♭) used?*

To indicate an intermediate tone the tendency from which is downward.

108. *For what is a cancel (♮) used?*

To cancel the effect of a previous sharp or flat.

109. *How many ways are there of representing each intermediate tone and what are they?*

Two: if its tendency is upward, it is represented by the lower of two degrees, modified, and called sharp; if its tendency is downward it is represented by the higher of two degrees, modified, and called flat.

NOTE 14.—There are exceptions to this as to all general rules.

110. *What is an interval?*

An interval is the difference of pitch between two tones, also the name given to the effect when they are performed simultaneously.

---

* The pernicious effects of calling this character (♮) a "NATURAL" are apparent throughout the entire country; notwithstanding the fact that, when so employed, its use is purely *technical*, it is very easy to see how readily the idea would obtain, in the minds of beginners, that some tones and keys are more natural than others; and the unfortunate impression which has become so universal among those who have little knowledge of the subject, that the key of O is more natural than other keys, and that the real difficulty in learning to read music only begins when we introduce other keys, is clearly traceable to the inappropriate name of this character. The character itself is never used except for the purpose of canceling the effect of a previous sharp or flat; hence, no instance can arise in which the word "*natural*" may be used where the word "CANCEL" would not be more appropriate. For these reasons the author has decided to adopt the name CANCEL instead; and would ask all teachers to assist in the effort to curtail the evil effects of the term *natural.*—H. R. P., New York, October 18, 1884.

111. *What is a prime?*

Prime is the name given to two tones which involve but one degree in representation, as C and C; a unison.

Ex. 40.   A Prime or Unison.

112. *What is a second?*

An interval which involves two degrees in representation, as C and D.

Ex. 41.   A Second.

113. *What is a third?*

An interval which involves three degrees in representation, as C and E.

Ex. 42.   A Third.

114. *What is a fourth?*

An interval which involves four degrees in representation, as C and F.

Ex. 43.   A Fourth.

115. *What is a fifth?*

An interval which involves five degrees in representation, as C and G.

Ex. 44.   A Fifth.

116. *What is a sixth?*

An interval which involves six degrees in representation, as C and A.

Ex. 45.   A Sixth.

117. *What is a seventh?*

An interval which involves seven degrees in representation, as C and B.

Ex. 46.   A Seventh.

118. *What is an octave?*

An interval which involves eight degrees in representation, as C and C eight degrees above.

Ex. 47. AN OCTAVE.

119. *What is a ninth?*

An interval which involves nine degrees in representation, as C and D nine degrees above.

Ex. 48. A NINTH.

120. *How are intervals measured?*

By means of steps and half-steps.

121. *What is a half-step?*

A half-step is the smallest measurement now in use.

122. *What is a step?*

A measurement as great as two half-steps.

NOTE 15.—The pupil should discriminate carefully between intervals (seconds, thirds, etc.) and their measurements (steps and half-steps). It would not be telling the *whole truth* to say "a half-step above C is D flat," for while D flat *is* a half-step from C, so is C sharp. The whole truth would be to say "from C to D flat is a minor second" (see Question 128 for explanation of minor second), which cannot possibly be said of C and C sharp. One might as well call for a "bushel basket" when he wants a "bushel of wheat." The interval is the wheat, the steps and half-steps are the basket with which it is measured.

123. *How many kinds of primes are there, and what are they called?*

Two; perfect primes and augmented primes.

124. *What is a perfect prime?*

Two tones on the same pitch; a unison.

125. *What is an augmented prime?*

A prime as great as a half-step.

Ex. 49. PRIMES.

Perfect. Augmented.

126. *How many kinds of seconds are there, and what are they called?*

Three; major seconds, minor seconds, and augmented seconds.

127. *What is a major second?*

A second as great as a step.

128. *What is a minor second?*

A second as small as a half-step.

129. *What is an augmented second?*

A second as great as a step-and-a-half.

Ex. 50. Seconds.

Major.   Minor.   Augmented.

130. *How many kinds of thirds are there, and what are they called?*

Three; major thirds, minor thirds and diminished thirds.

131. *What is a major third?*

A third as great as two steps.

132. *What is a minor third?*

A third as great as one step and one half-step.

133. *What is a diminished third?*

A third as small as two half-steps.

Ex. 51. Thirds.

Major.   Minor.   Diminished.

134. *How many kinds of fourths are there, and what are they called?*

Three; perfect, diminished and augmented.

135. *What is a perfect fourth?*

A fourth as great as two steps and one half-step.

136. *What is a diminished fourth?*

A fourth as great as one step and two half-steps.

137. *What is an augmented fourth?*

A fourth as great as three steps.

Ex. 52. Fourths.

Perfect.   Diminished.   Augmented.

138. *How many fifths are there, and what are they called?*

Three; perfect, diminished and augmented.

NOTE 16.—It will be noticed that the terms "major" and "minor" are applied to seconds, thirds, sixths and sevenths, but not to primes, octaves, fourths or fifths, these taking the term "perfect" instead. The reason for this will be given in detail in a future Primer, but may be shadowed forth here, as follows: Some intervals change their character by *inversion;* thus diminished intervals, when inverted, become augmented intervals; major intervals, when inverted, become minor intervals; but perfect intervals, when inverted, do not change their character, so to speak; hence the term "perfect." (See Remark 2, p. 35).

139. *What is a perfect fifth?*

A fifth as great as three steps and one half-step.

140. *What is a diminished fifth?*

A fifth as great as two steps and two half-steps.

141. *What is an augmented fifth?*

A fifth as great as two steps, one half-step and a step-and-a-half.

Ex. 53. Fifths.

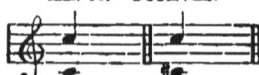

Perfect. Diminished. Augmented.

142. *How many sixths are there, and what are they called?*

Three; major, minor and augmented.

143. *What is a major sixth?*

A sixth as great as four steps and one half-step.

144. *What is a minor sixth?*

A sixth as great as three steps and two half-steps.

145. *What is an augmented sixth?*

A sixth as great as three steps, one half-step and a step-and-a-half

Ex. 54. Sixths.

Major. Minor. Augmented.

146. *How many kinds of sevenths are there, and what are they called?*

Three; major, minor and diminished.

147. *What is a major seventh?*

A seventh as great as five steps and one half-step.

148. *What is a minor seventh?*

A seventh as great as four steps and two half-steps.

149. *What is a diminished seventh?*

A seventh as great as three steps and three half-steps.

Ex. 55. Sevenths.

Major. Minor. Diminished.

150. *How many kinds of octaves are there, and what are they called?*

Two; perfect and diminished.

151. *What is a perfect octave?*

An octave as great as five steps and two half-steps.

152. *What is a diminished octave?*

An octave as great as four steps and three half-steps.

Ex. 56. Octaves.

Perfect. Diminished.

153. *How many kinds of ninths are there, and what are they called?*

Three; major, minor and augmented.

154. *What is a major ninth?*

A ninth as great as six steps and two half-steps; an octave and a major second.

155. *What is a minor ninth?*

A ninth as great as five steps and three half-steps; an octave and a minor second.

156. *What is an augmented ninth?*

A ninth as great as five steps, two half-steps and a step-and-a-half; an octave and an augmented second.

Ex. 57. NINTHS.

Major.   Minor.   Augmented.

157. *What is a chromatic half-step?*

A half-step which involves but one degree in representation, as C and C♯, A and A♭; an augmented prime.

158. *What is a diatonic half-step?*

A half-step involving two degrees in representation, as C and D♭, A and G♯; a minor second.

Ex. 58. CHROMATIC AND DIATONIC HALF STEPS.

Chromatic.   Diatonic.

159. *For what is a double sharp used?*

A double sharp is used for sharping a degree which has already been sharped by the signature or otherwise. (See Note 28, page 39.)

160. *How is a double sharp indicated?*

Usually by a cross thus ✕ or ✖ before a note.

NOTE 17.—In rare cases it is indicated by two sharps before a note, thus ♯♯.

161. *How is a double sharp contradicted?*

By a sharp with a cancel before it, thus ♮ ♯.

162. *For what is a double flat used?*

A double flat is used for flatting a degree which has already been flatted by the signature or otherwise.

163. *How is a double flat indicated?*

By two flats, thus ♭♭, before a note.

164. *How is a double flat contradicted?*

By a flat with a cancel before it, thus ♮ ♭.

CHAPTER VI.

MAJOR KEYS AND SCALES.

165. *What is a key?*

A key is a family of tones bearing certain fixed relations each to the others.

166. *How many tones constitute a key?*

Seven.

NOTE 18.—A key really consists of all the tones which the ear can detect as having the correct relations to each other; for example, all possible tones whose names are C, D, E, F, G, A and B, constitute the key of C, although the key is manifested by any seven of them.

167. *What is the tonic or key-tone?*

The tone from which all other tones are reckoned; the point of repose.

168. *How are the tones of a key named?*

The tonic or key-tone is named *one* (or *eight*), the next tone above it is named *two*, the next *three*, the next *four*, etc.

169. *What syllables are applied to the tones of a key?*

The syllable Do is applied to one, Re (*ray*) to two, Mi (*me*) to three, Fa (*fah*) to four, Sol to five, La (*lah*) to six, Si (*see*) to seven, and Do to eight (eight being one to all above it, takes the same syllable as one).*

NOTE 19.—The syllable names of tones are not presented here because the author expects them to be of any *practical* use to the piano pupil, but because every piano player should be more or less acquainted with vocal methods.

170. *What constitutes the diatonic scale?*

The tones of a key in successive order, from one key-tone, or tonic, to the next inclusive.

171. *What is the difference between a scale and a key?*

A scale implies a certain order of succession, *i. e.*, it *must* proceed

---

* In order to avoid the confusion which arises from giving the same syllable name to 7 (Si) of the major key, and 7 (Si) of the minor key, and the same name to flat 7 (Se) and flat 5 (Se) of the major key, the writer has decided to adopt the syllable Ti for 7 of the major key (flat 7 becoming Te), which obviates the difficulty completely, and he respectfully asks the aid and co-operation of all good teachers in these reforms in our musical nomenclature, as well as some others which will appear throughout the primer.—H. R. P.

step by step from one key-tone to the next, while the family of tones of which it is formed, called the key, may be used in any possible order.

NOTE 20.—It is to be regretted that the words *key* and *scale* are used as synonymous terms by many teachers, for, as will be perceived by a moment's reflection, a *scale* is one of the simplest little melodies which can be written in a key, and can never be varied, *i. e.*, it *must* always follow this ladder-like order, while the tones of a key may be used in an absolutely endless variety as regards order of succession; hence it is clear that a *scale* is a little thing when compared with a *key*, which is a great thing.

172. *What further difference is there between a scale and a key?*

A scale is not complete without eight tones, while a key is manifest with seven.

173. *How many key-modes are there, and what are they called?*

Two; major and minor.

174. *In what do they differ?*

In their thirds and sixths; in minor keys the thirds and sixths must be minor, while in major keys those intervals are major.

175. *What is the order of intervals in major scales?*

Major seconds must occur between 1 and 2, 2 and 3, 4 and 5, 5 and 6, and 6 and 7; minor seconds must occur between 3 and 4, and 7 and 8.

Ex. 59.   SCALE OF C MAJOR, ORDER OF INTERVALS.

Major.   Major.   Minor.   Major.   Major.   Major.   Minor.

176. *How many major keys are there in general use?*
Twelve.

177. *What tones form the key of C?*

C, D, E, F, G, A and B.

Ex. 60.   THE C SCALE.

With Bass Clef.   With Treble Clef.

178. *What is a signature?*

The sharps and flats at the beginning of a composition which indicate the key.

NOTE 21.—Hence the key of C has no signature; (see Webster's Dictionary).

179. *What tones form the key of G?*

G, A, B, C, D, E and F♯.

Ex. 61.   THE G SCALE.

With Bass Clef.   With Treble Clef.

180. *What is the signature of the key of G?*

One sharp.

NOTE 22.—The pupil will observe that the sharp in Example 61 is placed before **F**, and is limited in its effect, but if brought back to the beginning as in Example 62, it forms a SIGNATURE, and as such, modifies not only the degree of the staff on which it stands, but all its octaves above and below, throughout the entire composition, *i. e.*, all degrees which formerly represented **F**, now, by virtue of the signature, represent F♯.

Ex. 62. THE G SCALE WITH ITS PROPER SIGNATURE.

With Bass Clef. With Treble Clef.

181. *What tones form the key of D?*

D, E, F♯, G, A, B and C♯.

Ex. 63. THE D SCALE.

With Bass Clef. With Treble Clef.

182. *What is the signature of the key of D?*

Two sharps.

Ex. 64. THE D SCALE WITH ITS PROPER SIGNATURE.

With Bass Clef. With Treble Clef.

183. *What tones form the key of A?*

A, B, C♯, D, E, F♯ and G♯.

Ex. 65. THE A SCALE.

With Bass Clef. With Treble Clef.

184. *What is the signature of the key of A?*

Three sharps.

Ex. 66. THE A SCALE WITH ITS PROPER SIGNATURE.

With Bass Clef. With Treble Clef.

185. *What tones form the key of E?*

E, F♯, G♯, A, B, C♯ and D♯.

Ex. 67. THE E SCALE.

With Bass Clef. With Treble Clef.

186. *What is the signature of the key of E?*

Four sharps.

Ex. 68. The E Scale with its Proper Signature.

With Bass Clef.   With Treble Clef.

187. *What tones form the key of B?*

B, C♯, D♯, E, F♯, G♯ and A♯.

Ex. 69. The B Scale.

With Bass Clef.   With Treble Clef.

188. *What is the signature of the key of B?*

Five sharps.

Ex. 70. The B Scale with its Proper Signature.

With Bass Clef.   With Treble Clef.

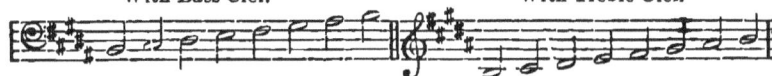

189. *What tones form the key of F♯?*

F♯, G♯, A♯, B, C♯, D♯ and E♯.

Ex. 71. The F♯ Scale.

With Bass Clef.   With Treble Clef.

Note 23.—It will be readily seen that although the pitch E♯ is identical with the pitch F, there are two reasons why it cannot be named or represented as F. *First*, the D degree of the staff, being used for 6, and the F degree for 7, the E degree would be left out; thus making the interval between 6 and 7 a third of some kind instead of a second; and *secondly*, the F degree being already used to represent 8, cannot be used to represent 7; for, although a degree can be made to represent two tones, a half-step, or even a step apart, it can, in *no possible manner*, be made to represent two tones, the interval between which is a major, or even a minor second. It should be remembered that the word *second* always implies *two degrees*, while the word step or half-step *may* or *may not* imply two degrees. Hence, those writers and teachers are wrong who adopt the language "from one to two is a step, from three to four is a half-step," etc. For instance, in the C scale, from E to E♯ (same pitch as F) is a half-step, but it is not a minor second.

190. *What is the signature of the key of F♯?*

Six sharps.

Ex. 72. The F♯ Scale with its Proper Signature.

With Bass Clef.   With Treble Clef.

191. *What tones form the key of C♯?*

C♯, D♯, E♯, F♯, G♯, A♯ and B♯.

Ex. 73. THE C♯ SCALE.

With Bass Clef.   With Treble Clef.

192. *What is the signature of the key of C♯?*
Seven sharps.

Ex. 74. THE C♯ SCALE WITH ITS PROPER SIGNATURE.

With Bass Clef.   With Treble Clef.

193. *What remarkable similarity is there between the scales of C♯ and D♭?*
They are both produced by pressing the same keys.

194. *What tones form the key of F?*
F, G, A, B♭, C, D and E.

Ex. 75. THE F SCALE.

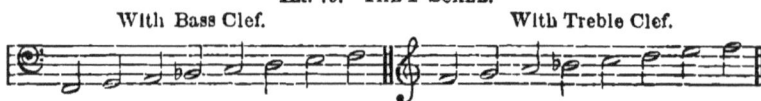

With Bass Clef.   With Treble Clef.

195. *What is the signature of the key of F?*
One flat.

Ex. 76. THE F SCALE WITH ITS PROPER SIGNATURE.

With Bass Clef.   With Treble Clef.

196. *What tones form the key of B♭?*
B♭, C, D, E♭, F, G and A.

Ex. 77. THE B♭ SCALE.

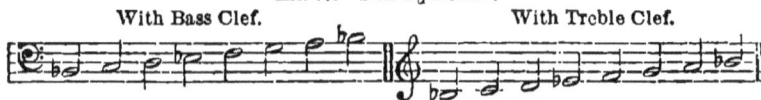

With Bass Clef.   With Treble Clef.

197. *What is the signature of the key of B♭?*
Two flats.

Ex. 78. THE B♭ SCALE WITH ITS PROPER SIGNATURE.

With Bass Clef.   With Treble Clef.

198. *What tones form the key of E♭?*
E♭, F, G, A♭, B♭, C and D.

Ex. 79.   The E♭ Scale.
With Bass Clef.   With Treble Clef.

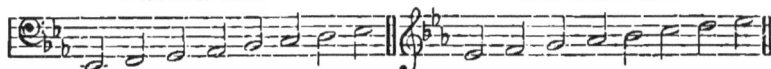

199. *What is the signature of the key of E♭?*
Three flats.

Ex. 80.   The E♭ Scale with its Proper Signature.
With Bass Clef.   With Treble Clef.

200. *What tones form the key of A♭?*
A♭, B♭, C, D♭, E♭, F and G.

Ex. 81.   The A♭ Scale.
With Bass Clef.   With Treble Clef.

201. *What is the signature of the key of A♭?*
Four flats.

Ex. 82.   The A♭ Scale with its Proper Signature.
With Bass Clef.   With Treble Clef.

202. *What tones form the key of D♭?*
D♭, E♭, F, G♭, A♭, B♭ and C.

Ex. 83.   The D♭ Scale.
With Bass Clef.   With Treble Clef.

203. *What is the signature of the key of D♭?*
Five flats.

Ex. 84.   The D♭ Scale with its Proper Signature.
With Bass Clef.   With Treble Clef.

204. What tones form the key of G♭ ?

G♭, A♭, B♭, C♭, D♭, E♭ and F.

Ex. 85. The G♭ Scale.

With Bass Clef.   With Treble Clef.

NOTE 24.—It will be noticed that although the pitch C♭ is identical with the pitch B, in this key, it cannot be called B in this key, for the B degree having been used for 3. (D♭), it must not be used for 4; moreover, if 4 should be represented on the B degree and 5 on the D degree (D♭), the interval between 4 and 5 would be a diminished third instead of a major second. Reperuse Note 23, page 31.

205. What is the signature of the key of G♭ ?

Six flats.

Ex. 86. The G♭ Scale with its Proper Signature.

With Bass Clef.   With Treble Clef.

206. What remarkable similarity is there in the scales of G♭ and F♯ ?

They are both produced by pressing the same keys

207. What tones form the key of C♭ ?

C♭, D♭, E♭, F♭, G♭, A♭ and B♭.

Ex. 87. The C♭ Scale.

With Bass Clef.   With Treble Clef.

208. What is the signature of the key of C♭ ?

Seven flats.

Ex. 88. The C♭ Scale with its Proper Signature.

With Bass Clef.   With Treble Clef.

209. What remarkable similarity is there between the scales of C♭ and B ?

They are both produced by pressing the same keys.

NOTE 25.—The following diagram shows the transposition of the Major Scales through the entire circle, both by sharps and by flats. In transposition by sharps read to the right: 5 of each scale becomes 1 of the scale which follows. In transposition by flats, read to the left: 4 of each scale becomes 8 of the scale which follows.

Ex. 89.   Transposition of Major Scales.

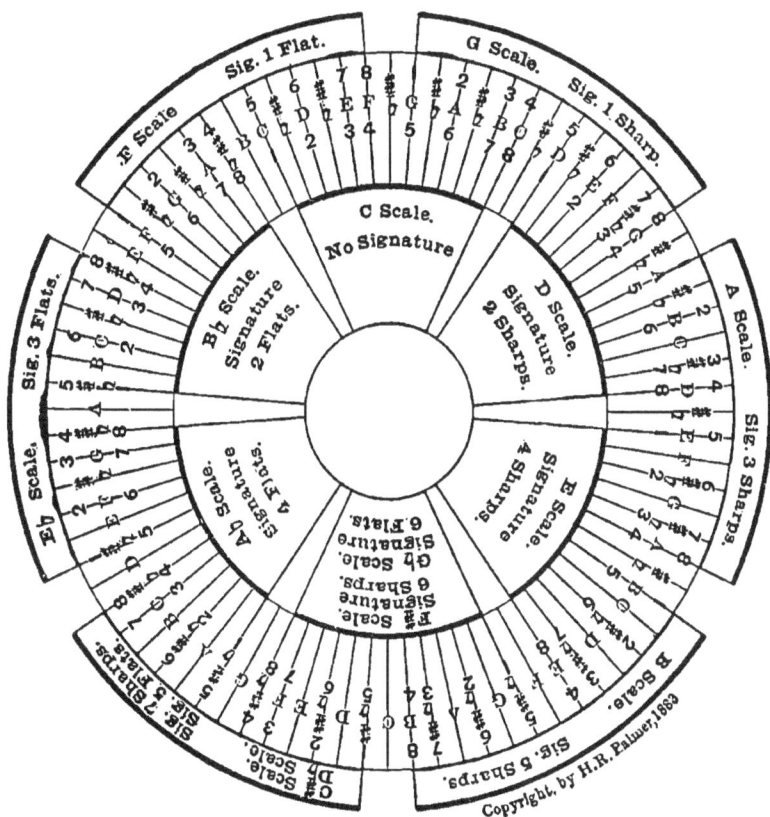

Remark 2.—Commenting on Note 16, Dr. Mason says: "C. F. Weitzmann has discarded the term 'perfect' fifth, and gives good reasons for so doing (see Bowman's Weitzmann, page 31, Wm. A. Pond & Co., N. Y.). Of course, your work must explain the musical terms as hitherto used, but I think it would also be well to take note of the advances and improvements of modern times."

CHAPTER VII.

MINOR KEYS AND SCALES.

210. *What is a minor key?*

A key in which the intervals from 1 to 3 and from 1 to 6 are minor.

211. *What is the order of intervals in minor scales?*

Major seconds must occur between 1 and 2, 3 and 4, and 4 and 5; minor seconds must occur between 2 and 3, 5 and 6, and 7 and 8; while from 6 to 7 must be an augmented second.

Ex. 90. SCALE OF A MINOR. ASCENDING.

Major.   Minor.   Major.   Major.   Minor. Augmented. Minor.

212. *Should this order of intervals be preserved in descending?*

It should.

Ex. 91. SCALE OF A MINOR. DESCENDING.

Minor. Augmented. Minor.   Major.   Major.   Minor.   Major.

213. *What is this form of the minor scale called?*

The harmonic minor scale.

214. *How is the harshness of the augmented second between 6 and 7 sometimes temporarily avoided?*

By "raising the sixth," or, more correctly speaking, by making the interval from 1 to 6 major instead of minor.

NOTE 26.—This avoidance of the augmented second between 6 and 7, by "raising 6," gave rise to what has been called the "Melodic Minor Scale," which is given by some writers, and still adhered to by many teachers. But the law which provides that all dominant chords shall have major thirds, and thus fixes 7 of the minor key a half-step below 8, is no more binding than the law which says that the sub-dominant chord of a minor key shall always have a minor third, and so establishes the interval of an augmented second from 6 to 7. It is absolutely impossible to harmonize the melodic form in any acceptable manner; and while all the classical composers frequently gave that form in melodic passages, they invariably wrote the sub-dominant chord with a minor third. Most of the old theorists pass over this striking inconsistency in silence; probably recognizing the fact that any attempt to reconcile such palpable contradictions would be utterly useless. Richter says that "The sixth degree of the minor scale (key) is not capable, *in a harmonic sense*, of any such chromatic alteration;" also, that the subdominant chord with a major third (in the minor key), "cannot be conceived of." In other words, we have but one minor *key*, that which has been known as the *Harmonic Minor* (the order of intervals of which is given at question 211), and while we frequently form a scale, called the Melodic Minor Scale, there *never was a Melodic Minor Key*. Whenever such passages occur, they can easily be accounted for as passing tones or appoggiaturas.

215. *A scale formed thus is called what?*
The melodic minor scale.

Ex. 92. The Melodic Minor Scale. Ascending.

Major.   Minor.   Major.   Major.   Major.   Major.   Minor.

216. *Should the same order of intervals be preserved in descending?*
It should not.

217. *What is the order of intervals in the melodic minor scale descending?*
From 8 to 7 and 7 to 6 must be major seconds; from 6 to 5 a minor second, 5 to 4 and 4 to 3 major seconds, 3 to 2 a minor second, and from 2 to 1 a major second.

Ex. 93. The Melodic Minor Scale. Descending.

Major.   Major.   Minor.   Major.   Major.   Minor.   Major.

Note 27.—To the indefinite manner in which the harmonic and melodic modes have been introduced in some of the popular piano instruction books, is to be traced the confused idea of minor scales which has obtained in the minds of many otherwise excellent teachers. For example, Richardson's Method only explains the harmonic mode in theory, while in practice, the melodic mode is used exclusively in ascending, and the harmonic mode as exclusively in descending. Thus·

Melodic mode.   Ex. 94.   Harmonic mode.

Had it been explained that the two modes were blended in such practice, all confusion would have been avoided.

218. *What is meant by relative major and relative minor?*
Each major key has its relative minor key, and each minor key has its relative major key. Six of each major key becomes one of its relative minor key, and three of each minor key becomes one of its relative major key—both keys having the same signature.

219. *What tones form the key of A minor?*
A, B, C, D, E, F, and G♯.

220. What is the signature of the key of A minor?
Like its relative, C major, it has no signature.

Ex. 95.   THE SCALE OF A MINOR (relativo of C major).

With Bass Clef.   With Treble Clef.

221. What tones form the key of E minor?
E, F♯, G, A, B, C, and D♯.
222. What is the signature of the key of E minor?
Like its relative, G major, its signature is one sharp.

Ex. 96.   THE SCALE OF E MINOR (relative of G major).

With Bass Clef.   With Treble Clef.

223. What tones form the key of B minor?
B, C♯, D, E, F♯, G, and A♯.
224. What is the signature of the key of B minor?
Like its relative, D major, its signature is two sharps.

Ex. 97.   THE SCALE OF B MINOR (relative of D major).

With Bass Clef.   With Treble Clef.

225. What tones form the key of F♯ minor?
F♯, G♯, A, B, C♯, D, and E♯.
226. What is the signature of the key of F♯ minor?
Like its relative, A major, its signature is three sharps.

Ex. 98.   THE SCALE OF F♯ MINOR (relative of A major).

With Bass Clef.   With Treble Clef.

227. What tones form the key of C♯ minor?
C♯, D♯, E, F♯, G♯, A, and B♯.
228. What is the signature of the key of C♯ minor?
Like its relative, E major, its signature is four sharps.

Ex. 99.   THE SCALE OF C♯ MINOR (relative of E major).

With Bass Clef.   With Treble Clef.

229. *What tones form the key of G♯ minor?*

G♯, A♯, B, C♯, D♯, E, and F double sharp (✕).

NOTE 28.—Although the pitch F double sharp is identical with the pitch G, it cannot here be named or represented as G, that degree being already occupied in representing 1 (or 8); moreover, E is 6, and if the G degree were used as 7, it would make the interval between 6 and 7 a third (*e. g.*), besides leaving the F degree out altogether; hence, we are compelled to modify the F degree with a double sharp (✕) and make it stand for the pitch 7.

230. *What is the signature of the key of G♯ minor?*

Like its relative, B major, its signature is five sharps.

Ex. 100. THE SCALE OF G♯ MINOR (relative of B major).

With Bass Clef.   With Treble Clef.

NOTE 29.—The key of G♯ major appears in the enharmonically related form of A♭ major (for meaning of the term enharmonic, see foot-note on page 45).

231. *What tones form the key of D♯ minor?*

D♯, E♯, F♯, G♯, A♯, B, and C double sharp.

232. *What is the signature of the key of D♯ minor?*

Like its relative, F♯ major, its signature is six sharps.

Ex. 101. THE SCALE OF D♯ MINOR (relative of F♯ major).

With Bass Clef.   With Treble Clef.

NOTE 30.—The key of D♯ major appears in the enharmonically related form of E♭ major.

233. *What tones form the key of D minor?*

D, E, F, G, A, B♭, and C♯.

234. *What is the signature of the key of D minor?*

Like its relative, F major, its signature is one flat.

Ex. 102. THE SCALE OF D MINOR (relative of F major).

With Bass Clef.   With Treble Clef.

235. *What tones form the key of G minor?*

G, A, B♭, C, D, E♭, and F♯.

236. *What is the signature of the key of G minor?*

Like its relative, B♭ major, its signature is two flats.

Ex. 103. THE SCALE OF G MINOR (relative of B♭ major).

With Bass Clef.   With Treble Clef.

237. *What tones form the key of C minor?*

C, D, E♭, F, G, A♭, and B.

238. *What is the signature of the key of C minor?*

Like its relative, E♭ major, its signature is three flats.

EX. 104.   THE SCALE OF C MINOR (relative of E♭ major).

With Bass Clef.   With Treble Clef.

239. *What tones form the key of F minor?*

F, G, A♭, B♭, C, D♭, and E.

240. *What is the signature of the key of F minor?*

Like its relative, A♭ major, its signature is four flats.

EX. 105.   THE SCALE OF F MINOR (relative of A♭ major).

With Bass Clef.   With Treble Clef.

241. *What tones form the key of B♭ minor?*

B♭, C, D♭, E♭, F, G♭, and A.

242. *What is the signature of the key of B♭ minor?*

Like its relative, D♭ major, its signature is five flats.

EX. 106.   THE SCALE OF B♭ MINOR (relative of D♭ major).

With Bass Clef.   With Treble Clef.

243. *What tones form the key of E♭ minor?*

E♭, F, G♭, A♭, B♭, C♭, and D.

244. *What is the signature of the key of E♭ minor?*

Like its relative, G♭ major, its signature is six flats.

EX. 107.   THE SCALE OF E♭ MINOR (relative of G♭ major).

With Bass Clef.   With Treble Clef.

245. *What remarkable similarity is there in the scales of E♭ minor and D♯ minor?*

They are both produced by pressing the same keys.

NOTE 31.—The following diagram shows the transposition of the Minor Scales through the entire circle, both by sharps and by flats. In transposition by sharps, read to the right: 5 of each scale becomes 1 of the scale which follows. In transposition by flats, read to the left: 4 of each scale becomes 8 of the scale which follows.

Ex. 108. TRANSPOSITION OF MINOR SCALES.

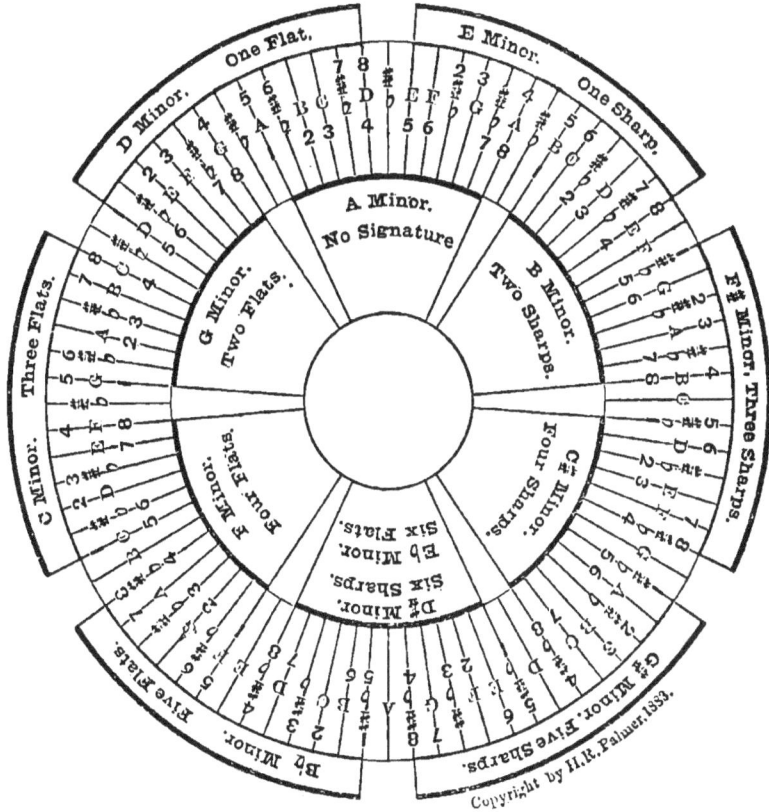

NOTE 32.—Below are represented the several TONICS or KEY-TONES, together with their respective signatures. The large notes represent ONE (Do) of the major key; and the smaller notes represent ONE (La) of the relative minor key.

Ex. 109.

Key of C. | Key of G. | Key of D. | Key of A. | Key of E. | Key of B. | Key of F♯.

One.   One.   One.   One.   One.   One.   One.

Key of F. | Key of B♭. | Key of E♭. | Key of A♭. | Key of D♭. | Key of G♭.

One.   One.   One.   One.   One.   One.

NOTE 33.—In the following tables we present a bird's-eye view of the several transpositions in great detail.

MAJOR KEYS.

Ex. 109.

TRANSPOSITION BY SHARPS.

Note	No Signature	One Sharp	Two Sharps	Three Sharps	Four Sharps	Five Sharps	Six Sharps
C							
B						8 Do	
a#						7 Si	
A				8 Do			
g#				7 Si	6 La		
G		8 Do					
f#		7 Si		6 La	5 Sol	8 Do	
F						7 Si	
E		6 La		5 Sol	8 Do	4 Fa	
d#					7 Si	3 Mi	6 La
D		5 Sol	8 Do	4 Fa			
c#			7 Si	3 Mi	6 La	2 Re	5 Sol
C	8 Do	4 Fa					
B	7 Si	3 Mi	6 La	2 Re	5 Sol	1 Do	4 Fa
a#							3 Mi
A	5 La	2 Re	5 Sol	1 Do	4 Fa		
g#					3 Mi		2 Re
G	5 Sol	1 Do	4 Fa				
f#			3 Mi		2 Re		1 Do
F	4 Fa						
E	3 Mi		2 Re		1 Do		
d#							
D	2 Re		1 Do				
c#							
C	1 Do						
	Key of C	Key of G	Key of D	Key of A	Key of E	Key of B	Key of F#

TRANSPOSITION BY FLATS.

Note	One Flat	Two Flats	Three Flats	Four Flats	Five Flats	Six Flats	Note
C							C
B							B
a#	8 Do						bb
A	7 Si						A
g#			8 Do				ab
G	6 La		7 Si				G
f#					8 Do		gb
F	8 Do	5 Sol		6 La	7 Si		F
E	7 Si						E
d#		4 Fa	8 Do	5 Sol		6 La	eb
D	6 La	3 Mi	7 Si				D
c#				4 Fa	8 Do	5 Sol	db
C	5 Sol	2 Re	6 La	3 Mi	7 Si		C
B						4 Fa	B
a#	4 Fa	1 Do	5 Sol	2 Re	6 La	3 Mi	bb
A	3 Mi						A
g#			4 Fa	1 Do	5 Sol	2 Re	ab
G	2 Re		3 Mi				G
f#					4 Fa	1 Do	gb
F	1 Do		2 Re		3 Mi		F
E							E
d#				1 Do		2 Re	eb
D							D
c#						1 Do	db
C							C
Key of F	Key of Bb	Key of Eb	Key of Ab	Key of Db	Key of Gb		

MINOR KEYS.

Ex. 110.

TRANSPOSITION BY SHARPS.

	No Signature	Signature One Sharp	Signature Two Sharps	Signature Three Sharps	Signature Four Sharps	Signature Five Sharps	Signature Six Sharps	
A								A
G#						8 La		
G						7 Si		G
F#				8 La				
F				7 Si				F
E		8 La				5 Fa		E
D#		7 Si				5 Mi	8 La	
D			6 Fa				7 Si	D
C#			5 Mi	8 La		4 Re		
C		6 Fa		7 Si				C
B		5 Mi	8 La	4 Re	3 Do	6 Fa		B
A#			7 Si		2 Si	5 Mi		
A	8 La	4 Re		3 Do	6 Fa			A
G#	7 Si		2 Si	5 Mi	1 La	4 Re		
G		3 Do	6 Fa					G
F#		2 Si	5 Mi	1 La	4 Re	3 Do		
F	6 Fa					2 Si		F
E	5 Mi	1 La	4 Re		3 Do			E
D#					2 Si	1 La		
D	4 Re		3 Do					D
C#			2 Si		1 La			
C	3 Do							C
B	2 Si		1 La					B
A#								
A	1 La							A
	Key of A Minor.	Key of E Minor.	Key of B Minor.	Key of F# Minor.	Key of C# Minor.	Key of G# Minor.	Key of D# Minor.	

TRANSPOSITION BY FLATS.

	Signature One Flat	Signature Two Flats	Signature Three Flats	Signature Four Flats	Signature Five Flats	Signature Six Flats	
A							A
							a♭
G		8 La					G
		7 Si					g♭
F				8 La			F
E				7 Si			E
		6 Fa				8 La	e♭
D	8 La	5 Mi				7 Si	D
	7 Si			6 Fa			d♭
C			4 Re	8 La	5 Mi		C
B			7 Si			6 Fa	B
	6 Fa	3 Do		4 Re	8 La	5 Mi	b♭
A	5 Mi	2 Si			7 Si		A
			6 Fa	3 Do		4 Re	a♭
G	4 Re	1 La	5 Mi	2 Si			G
					6 Fa	3 Do	g♭
F	3 Do		4 Re	1 La	5 Mi	2 Si	F
E	2 Si						E
			3 Do		4 Re	1 La	e♭
D	1 La		2 Si				D
				3 Do			d♭
C		1 La		2 Si			C
B							B
						1 La	b♭
A							A
	Key of D Minor.	Key of G Minor.	Key of C Minor.	Key of F Minor.	Key of B♭ Minor.	Key of E♭ Minor.	

CHAPTER VIII.

LEADING-TONES.

246. *What is meant by leading-tone ?*

Seven of a key ; the tone which is a minor second below the tonic.

247. *What is the leading-tone in the key of C major.*

B.

248. *In its relative, A minor ?*

G♯.

249. *What is the leading-tone in the key of G major ?*

F♯.

250. *In its relative, E minor ?*

D♯.

251. *What is the leading-tone in the key of D major ?*

C♯.

252. *In its relative, B minor ?*

A♯.

253. *What is the leading-tone in the key of A major ?*

G♯.

254. *In its relative, F♯ minor ?*

E♯.

255. *What is the leading-tone in the key of E major ?*

D♯.

256. *In its relative, C♯ minor ?*

B♯.

257. *What is the leading-tone in the key of B major ?*

A♯.

258. *In its relative, G♯ minor ?*

F double sharp (✕).

259. *What is the leading-tone in the key of F♯ major?*
E♯.

260. *In its relative, D♯ minor?*
C double sharp (✕).

261. *What is the leading-tone in the key of F major?*
E.

262. *In its relative, D minor?*
C♯.

263. *What is the leading-tone in the key of B♭ major?*
A.

264. *In its relative, G minor?*
F♯.

265. *What is the leading-tone in the key of E♭ major?*
D.

266. *In its relative, C minor?*
B.

267. *What is the leading-tone in the key of A♭ major?*
G.

268. *In its relative, F minor?*
E.

269. *What is the leading-tone of the key of D♭ major?*
C.

270. *In its relative, B♭ minor?*
A.

271. *What is the leading-tone in the key of G♭ major?*
F.

272. *In its relative, E♭ minor?*
D.

NOTE 34.—The following tabulated form of showing the relative minor keys, with their leading-tones, may be useful for reference:

The relative of						leading-tone is			
"	"	"	C major is	A	minor;	"	"	"	G♯.
"	"	"	G "	E	" ;	"	"	"	D♯.
"	"	"	D "	B	" ;	"	"	"	A♯.
"	"	"	A "	F♯	" ;	"	"	"	E♯.
"	"	"	E "	C♯	" ;	"	"	"	B♯.
"	"	"	B "	G♯	" ;	"	"	"	F✕.
"	"	"* {	F♯ "	D♯ } *	" ;	"	"	"	C✕.
"	"	" {	G♭ "	E♭ }	" ;	"	"	"	D.
"	"	"	D♭ "	B♭	" ;	"	"	"	A.
"	"	"	A♭ "	F	" ;	"	"	"	E.
"	"	"	E♭ "	C	" ;	"	"	"	B.
"	"	"	B♭ "	G	" ;	"	"	"	F♯.
"	"	"	F "	D	" ;	"	"	"	C♯.

* Enharmonic, *i. e.*, a change of name, representation and resolution (tendency), without changing the tone itself.

The following is a table of relative major keys, with their leading-tones:

The relative of	A minor is C	major;	leading-tone is B.
" " "	E " " G	" ;	" " " F♯.
" " "	B " " D	" ;	" " " C♯.
" " "	F♯ " " A	" ;	" " " D♯.
" " "	C♯ " " E	" ;	" " " D♯.
" " "	G♯ " " B	" ;	" " " A♯.
" " " * { D♯ " " F♯ } *	" ;	" " " E♯.
" " " { E♭ " " G♭ }	" ;	" " " F.
" " "	B♭ " " D♭	" ;	" " " C.
" " "	F " " A♭	" ;	" " " G.
" " "	C " " E♭	" ;	" " " D.
" " "	G " " B♭	" ;	" " " A.
" " "	D " " F	" ;	" " " E.

273. *As a major key and its relative minor key have the same signature, how are we to know whether the piece is written in major or minor?*

If its first and last chords are major, and the final chord of most of its cadences is major, the piece is written in the major key; but if its first chord is minor and most of its cadences, especially the final one, end with minor chords, the piece is written in a minor key.

NOTE 35.—A chord is a combination of two or more tones, so arranged as to form the intervals of third and fifth from a fundamental tone. If the *third* is a major third, and the fifth is perfect, the chord is called a *major chord.* If the *third* is minor (with perfect fifth), the chord is called a *minor chord.* Chords (sometimes called Triads) are said to be *Augmented, Major, Minor* and *Diminished,* thus:—

Aug. Maj. Min. Dim.

The chords in the major and minor keys are as follows:—

Major Key.   Minor Key.

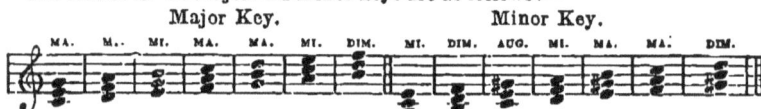

MA. M.. MI. MA. MA. MI. DIM. MI. DIM. AUG. MI. MA. MA. DIM.

When the fundamental tone of a chord (the tone from which the chord is named), is *lowest*, the chord is said to be in its *direct form ;* when the 3d of the chord is lowest, the chord is said to be in its *first inverted form* (or 1st inversion); if the fifth be lowest, it is in its *second inverted form* (or 2d inversion), thus:—

Chords of C.   Chords of A.
Direct. 1st In. 2d In. Direct. 1st In. 2d In.

Four-fold chords, or *chords of the seventh,* consist of four tones, viz : a *fundamental, third, fifth* and *seventh.* Their inversions follow the same order as those of the three-fold chords or *triads*, thus:—

Key of C Major.   Key of A Minor.
Chords of the Seventh of G. Chords of the Seventh of E.
Direct. 1st In. 2d In. 3d In. Direct. 1st In. 2d In. 3d In.

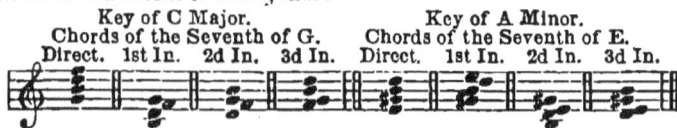

It is not thought best to elaborate the subject of chord formations here, as it more properly belongs to the department of "Thorough Base," and will be extensively treated in the author's "Thorough-Base Primer," which is expected to follow the present work.

* Enharmonic, *i. e.*, a change of name, representation and resolution (tendency), without changing the tone itself.

CHAPTER IX.

CHROMATIC SCALE, ACCIDENTALS, DEGREES OF POWER, Etc.

274. *What is a chromatic scale ?*

A scale in which all the tones, intermediate and diatonic, occur in successive order.

275. *Why is this scale called chromatic ?*

From the Greek word Χρῶμα (chroma), color; the intermediate tones were formerly written in colors; the ancient lyre divided the octave into thirteen tones and had colored strings.

276. *How is the chromatic scale formed ?*

By starting from any given tone and proceeding by half-steps to its octave, either upward or downward.

277. *How is the chromatic scale commonly written ?*

In ascending, the intermediate tones are generally indicated by sharps; in descending, by flats.

Ex. 110.   THE CHROMATIC SCALE.

Ascending (by sharps).

Descending (by flats).

NOTE 36.—As the chromatic scale embraces *all* keys, it cannot be said to be in any key.

278. *What are accidentals ?*

The sharps, flats or cancels used throughout a composition for the purpose of introducing intermediate tones.

279. *What is the rule for their continuance?*

Accidentals continue their significance throughout the measure in which they occur.

NOTE 37.—The following example will show the force of this rule of continuance. At (*a*) all the notes on the D degree are affected by the accidental ;

Ex. 111.

while at (*b*), although other notes intervene, still all the notes on the C degree are affected. It was formerly the practice to extend the influence of an accidental to all notes of the same letter-name in the measure, in whatever octave they might occur, as at (*c*) below ; however, modern composers would write the example as at (*d*).

Ex. 112.

But most confusing was the additional clause of this rule for the continuance of accidentals, namely : "And from measure to measure until canceled by an intervening note on another degree of the staff." Thus at (*e*) below, the D degree in the second measure was affected by the sharp in the first measure.

Ex. 113.

In explaining the following passage, (*g*), some would insist that D♯ occurs four times, while others would contend that only the first two notes are affected.

Ex. 114.

Fortunately, it is now the prevailing custom to place an accidental in the next measure whenever it is wanted, thus avoiding much annoyance

Sometimes it is desirable to cancel the effect of an accidental within the measure in which it occurs; this is done by a cancel as at (*h*) and (*j*) in the following example :

Ex. 115.

280. *What are* PASSING TONES ?

Tones that are introduced for the purpose of enlivening or embellishing the melody, but which do not form an essential part of the harmony.

Ex. 116. Passing Tones.

Essential tones of the melody.   The same with Passing tones.

281. *What is an* Appoggiatura ?

A passing tone which precedes an essential tone on an accented pulse of a measure.

282. *How is it usually represented ?*

By a smaller note.

Ex. 117. The Appoggiatura.

Written.   Performed.

Note 38.—Modern composers usually write out such passages in full. However, an intelligent reading of the old masters presupposes a knowledge of the Appoggiatura as explained above.

283. *What is an* Acciaccatura ?

A passing tone usually a half-step above or below the tone to which it is prefixed.

284. *How is it expressed ?*

By a small note with a dash across its hook.

285. *How should it be performed ?*

It has no determined time-value and should be closely blended with the following tone.

Note 39.—The meaning of the word Acciaccatura (*to crush*) gives a good idea of the way in which it should be performed.

Ex. 118. The Acciaccatura.

286. *What is an* After-Tone ?

A passing tone which follows an essential tone.

Ex. 119. The After-Tone.

Written.   Performed.

Note 40.—More extended explanations concerning these different kinds of passing tones, will be given in Chapter XI.

287. *How many degrees of power are there in common use?*

Five: Pianissimo, Piano, Mezzo, Forte and Fortissimo.

288. *What does pianissimo mean?*

That the tone or passage thus marked should be performed with great restraint; the first degree of power.

289. *How is pianissimo indicated?*

By double-p (*pp.*).

290. *What does piano mean?*

That the tone or passage so marked should be performed with restraint; the second degree of power.

291. *How is piano expressed?*

By the letter p (*p.*).

292. *What does mezzo mean?*

That the tone or passage should be performed with medium power, neither with restraint nor with uncommon exertion; the third degree of power.

293. *What does forte mean?*

That the tone or passage should be performed with some exertion; the fourth degree of power.

294. *What does fortissimo mean?*

That the tone or passage should be performed with great exertion, the loudest that can be given consistent with purity; the fifth degree of power.

Ex. 120. THE FIVE DEGREES OF POWER.

295. *What does crescendo mean?*

That the tone or passage should be commenced in a low degree of power and increased.

Ex. 121. CRESCENDO.

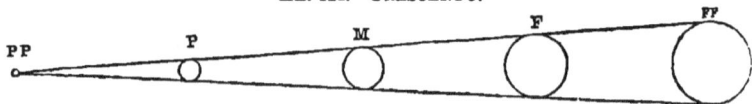

296. *What does decrescendo or diminuendo mean?*

That the tone or passage should be commenced in a high degree of power and decreased.

Ex. 122. DECRESCENDO.

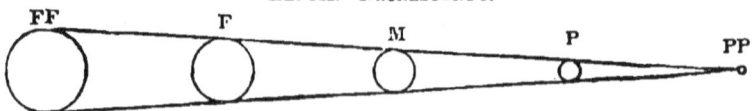

NOTE 41.—These five degrees of power are sufficient for all practical purposes, and if composers would grade them in this way, performers would soon learn to use them so. That there is an innumerable number of degrees of power between pianissimo and piano must be admitted, otherwise no such effect as crescendo could be produced, but like the innumerable number of pitches which, all must admit, lie between C and C♯, the human mind cannot classify or analyze them.

After many years' experience in conducting large bands of performers, both vocal and instrumental, the writer is prepared to assert, without fear of contradiction, that no performer can produce a degree of power between *piano* and *mezzo*, or between *mezzo* and *forte* (any more than he can produce a pitch between C and C♯); hence the terms *mezzo-piano* and *mezzo-forte*, with their abbreviations *m. p.* and *m. f.*, are nonsensical, and should be thrown out of our nomenclature. We might as well say *mezzo-pianissimo* or *mezzo-fortissimo*. The bad effects which have arisen from a lack of a classification of these degrees of power are shown by the fact that when our modern composers wish a passage to be performed *pianissimo*, they mark it with three or even with four *p*'s. Now, as *pianissimo* means that the tone or passage shall be as soft as possible, we cannot make it softer with a dozen *p*'s; and if *fortissimo* means all the power of which the performer is capable (consistent with pure tone), a thousand *f*'s would not make it louder.

297. *What does swell mean?*

A union of crescendo and diminuendo.

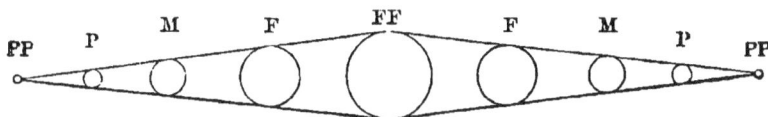

EX. 123. THE SWELL.

298. *What does sforzando mean?*

· That the tone should be forcibly commenced in a high degree of power, and instantly diminished and held in a low degree of power.

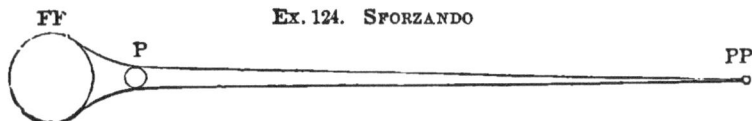

EX. 124. SFORZANDO

NOTE 42.—On the piano-forte the pure sforzando is impossible, but the *mental desire* to attain it produces a special attack, which is accepted in the place of the effect. Another way of indicating sforzando is *fp*. This is much used in German music, and almost exclusively in military band writing.—C. F.

CHAPTER X.

THE METRONOME; BEATING, COUNTING, Etc.

299. *By what means are we assisted in giving the correct time to each pulse of a measure?*

By means of a metronome; also by beating or counting the time.

300. *Describe a metronome.*

Metronome is from two Greek words, ηἔτρον, *a measure,* and νεμειν, *a law;* it distributes the time equally, by means of clockwork acting upon an inverted pendulum, to which is attached a sliding weight. Back of the pendulum is a graduated scale of numbers. The sliding weight being placed against a number, the metronome will give as many ticks per minute as are indicated by that number, thus:— M. M. (Maelzel's Metronome) ♩ = 60, means that the top of the sliding weight being placed at 60, there will be 60 ticks in a minute, each tick indicating the time of a half-note.

NOTE 43.—A more simple and inexpensive contrivance, and at the same time equally reliable, is the following : Attach a small weight to the end of a common tape measure which has the inches, with the halves, quarters and eighths marked upon it (such as is used by tailors will be found convenient). The greater the length, the slower will be the vibrations. To ascertain the movement of a piece of music marked ♩ = 60, hold the tape so that 39½ inches remain free; the vibrations will then indicate the time of a quarter note, as the metronome when set at 60.

In the following table the first column gives the metronome marks, and the second column gives the length of tape required.

Met.	Inches.	Met.	Inches.	Met.	Inches.	Met.	Inches.
50 =	565/8	66 =	317/8	92 =	163/4	120 =	91/4
52 =	511/2	69 =	297/8	96 =	151/2	126 =	81/2
54 =	483/8	72 =	263/4	100 =	143/8	132 =	73/4
56 =	453/8	76 =	243/4	104 =	133/8	138 =	71/4
58 =	421/4	80 =	213/8	108 =	123/8	144 =	65/8
60 =	391/2	84 =	195/8	112 =	113/8	152 =	61/8
63 =	35	88 =	181/2	116 =	101/4	180 =	51/8

301. *What is beating time?*

Indicating each pulsation of a measure by a certain motion of the hand or *baton* (a conducting-stick).

302. *Describe the beats in double measure.*

Down and up.

303. *Describe the beats in triple measure.*

Down, left, and up; or down, *right*, and up.

NOTE 44.—Most modern conductors seem to prefer down, *right*, and up, in triple measure, notwithstanding the fact that it upsets a rule which holds good throughout all other kinds of measure, viz.: "the *right beat* always indicates an accented pulse."

304. *Describe the beats in quadruple measure.*

Down, left, right, and up.

305. *Describe the beats in sextuple measure.*

Down, left, left, right, up, and up; or, in quicker movements, simply down and up, mentally dividing each beat into three pulses.

306. *Describe the beats in compound triple measure.*

Down, left, and up, or down, right, and up, mentally dividing each beat into three pulses.

307. *Describe the beats in compound quadruple measure.*

Down, left, right, and up, mentally dividing each beat into three pulses.

308. *What is counting time?*

Counting time is giving a short, energetic count to each pulse of a measure at equal intervals of time, like the ticking of a metronome or a clock.

309. *How is $\frac{2}{4}$ measure counted?*

A count is given to each quarter note or its equivalent, thus:—

Ex. 125.

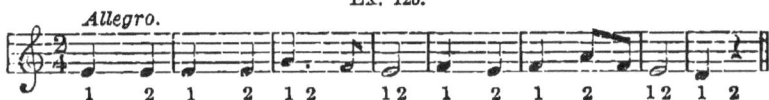

NOTE 45.—In slow movements, however, it is better to count four eighth notes in a measure, thus:—

Ex. 126.

310. *How is $\frac{3}{4}$ measure counted?*

A count is given to each quarter note or its equivalent, thus:—

Ex. 127.

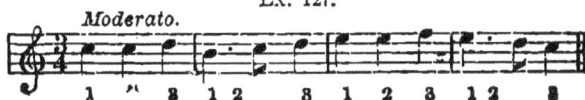

NOTE 46.—However, in slow movements it is better to count six eighth notes in a measure, thus:—

Ex. 128.

311. *How is* $\frac{4}{4}$ *measure counted?*

A count is given to each quarter note or its equivalent, thus:—

Ex. 129.

NOTE 47.—In slow movements it is better to count eight eighth notes in a measure, thus:—

Ex. 130.

312. *How is* $\frac{6}{8}$ *measure counted?*

In rapid movements a count is given to each dotted quarter note or its equivalent, thus:—

Ex. 131.

NOTE 48.—In slow movements, however, it is better to count six eighth notes in a measure, thus:—

Ex. 132.

313. *How is* $\frac{9}{8}$ *measure counted?*

A count is given to each dotted quarter note or its equivalent, thus:—

Ex. 133.

314. How is $1\frac{2}{8}$ *measure counted?*

A count is given to each dotted quarter note or its equivalent, thus :—

Ex. 134.

NOTE 49.—"In slow movements it is profitable to have the student subdivide the counts, *e. g.*, in the introduction of Beethoven's Sonata Pathetique, and in the Fifth Fugue in D (Bach's Well-tempered Clavichord). I frequently have pupils count 16 in a measure. On the other hand, in many quick pieces, I have them count the measures in groups (one to each measure), which frequently gives the real pulsation, *e. g.*, Chopin's Scherzi, where the study of rhythm in groups of four measures counting only *one* to each measure, at once clears up much of the composer's meaning, which is otherwise indistinct to many students."—W. H. S.

REMARK. Page 47, Note 36. Every Key (i, e, signature) contains two chromatic scales viz: one in the major mode of that signature, and one in the minor mode. For example: the major mode of the primary key (without signature) comprises four triads, viz: major tonic triad (C-e-G.), major dominant (G-b-D.), and either major or minor sub dominant, (F-a-C. or f, A flat-c.)

Thus, besides the seven primary tones implied by the major tonic triad (C-major), the major dominant (G-major) implies f#, the major sub dominant (F-major) implies b flat, and the minor sub dominant (f-minor) implies b-flat, e flat, a flat and d flat. Here, accordingly, there is all requisite material for a chromatic scale exclusively of tones directly affiliated with C-major thus:—

(ASCENDING & DESCENDING ALIKE.)

The four triads of the minor mode of the primitive key (without signature) are, minor tonic (a-C-e), minor sub dominant (d-F-a) and either minor dominant (primitive minor mode, e-G-b), or major dominant (modern minor, E-g#-B). The minor tonic (a-minor) implies seven primary tones, the minor sub dominant,(d-F-a) implies b flat, the minor dominant(e-G-b,) implies f#, and the the major dominant (E-g#-B) implies f#, c#, g# and d#. Hence the chromatic scale of the minor mode of the primary key (without signature) i, e, a minor :—

(ASCENDING & DESCENDING ALIKE.)

Similarly, the three major, and one minor triads of the major mode of the key of three sharps, yield the following chromatic scale of A major:—

(ASCENDING & DESCENDING ALIKE.)

And the three minor and one major, triads of the minor mode of the key of three sharps, yield the following chromatic scale of F sharp minor:--

(ASCENDING & DESCENDING ALIKE.)

The aid to the easy harmonization and singing of the chromatic scale in any of the major or minor modes, which is afforded by this derivation of the tone-names from the fundamental triads of the mode in which each particular scale occurs, is obvious, since the notation is always brought into intelligible relations to the true signature and tonic of the place where the scale occurs.—A. R. P.

CHAPTER XI.

THE TURN, TRILL, AND OTHER GRACES.

315. *How is a chord to be played when it has a waved line drawn per pendicularly before it?*

The tones of the chord are to be played in rapid succession from the lowest one; all are to be held until the last one is left.

Ex. 135.

Written.   Performed.

316. *How many different ways are there of introducing a* TURN *(some-times called* GRUPPETTO*), and what are they?*

Four: The Plain Turn; the Inverted Turn; the Turn when the sign is between two notes, and the Turn on a dotted note.

317. *How many different tones are used in every turn?*

Three: The principal tone; the tone one degree above it, and the tone one degree below it.

318. *How is the Plain Turn made?*

First, play the tone above; second, the principal tone; third, the tone below; and fourth, the principal tone.

319. *How do we determine whether the tone above and the tone below are to be distant a major second, or only a minor second?*

By the signature; *e. g.*, if in the key of C, a turn is marked over B, we would commence on C; but if the signature were two sharps, with a turn marked over B, we would begin on C♯. The tone below the principal tone is usually a minor second distant, except in the old masters (down to Bach), who were particular to indicate every accidental occurring in an ornament.

Ex. 136. THE PLAIN TURN.

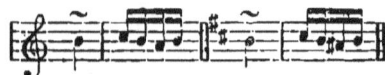

Written. Performed. Written. Performed.

320. *How is the Inverted Turn made?*

The Inverted Turn is the reverse of the Plain Turn; *i. e.*, we commence with the tone below instead of with the tone above.

Ex. 137.   THE INVERTED TURN.

321. *How do composers determine which of these Turns to write?*

In ascending passages the Plain Turn is generally used; in descending passages it is more customary to use the Inverted Turn.

Ex. 138.   THE TURN IN ASCENDING PASSAGES.

Written.   Performed.

Ex. 139.   THE TURN IN DESCENDING PASSAGES.

Written.   Performed.

NOTE 50.—There are many exceptions to this rule.

322. *When the sign is placed between two notes, how are we to play the turn?*

The preceding tone must be regarded as the principal, and is to be struck before the turn is begun, dividing the time equally with the turn.

Ex. 140.   THE TURN WHEN THE SIGN IS BETWEEN TWO NOTES.

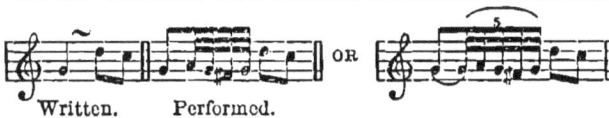

Written.   Performed.   OR

323. *How is the Turn on a Dotted Note made?*

The principal tone is played first, then the turn, as a triplet, bringing the principal tone again on the dot; the dotted note should be divided into three units of time: the first is given to the principal tone, the second to a triplet turn, and the third to the principal tone.

Ex. 141.   THE TURN ON A DOTTED NOTE.

Written.   Performed.

NOTE 51.—When the highest tone in a turn is a major second above the principal tone, the lowest tone is usually a minor second below the principal tone, and whether the chromatic sign is included, thus, $\widetilde{\sharp}$, or not, it should generally be played so, although much old music, notably Bach, seems to differ, frequently calling for a *major second* between the principal tone and the tone below ; but if the highest tone is a *minor second* above the principal tone, the lowest tone should usually be a *major second* below the principal tone, unless there is some indication to the contrary, thus :—

Ex. 142.

(a)   (b)   (c)   (d)   (e)   (f)   (g)   (h)

The turn at (a) should just as surely consist of A, G, F♯, G, as though expressly indicated, as at (e) ; at (b) the turn should take F♯, G, A, G, whether the sign calls for F♯ or not, as at (f). On the other hand, the turn at (c) should consist of the tones F, E, D, E, unless D♯ is expressly called for, as at (g) ; and at (d) the turn should take A, B, C, B, unless A♯ is indicated, as at (h).

Sometimes the turn-sign has a dash through it, thus, ~, in which case the principal tone must precede the turn.

Ex. 143.

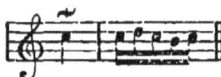

Written. Performed.

After all that can be said concerning the turn, the fact remains that composers are apt to use them very loosely, relying largely upon the taste of the performer. Modern composers, however, are inclined to notate their exact meaning, which is far better.

324. *How is the* TRILL *performed?*

The same as the Plain Turn, except that the *first two* tones are repeated, in equal succession, during the principal part of the time-value of the note, ending with the *last two* tones of the turn ; the whole should be as rapid as the ability of the performer will permit.

NOTE 52.—"In somber or heavy strains, I think there should be a comparatively *slow trill*. I generally have to teach them *slow* for years, in order to secure good quality, clear execution and distinctness. Most players trill too indefinitely."
—W. H. S.

Ex. 144. THE TRILL.

Written.   Performed.   *Turn.*

NOTE 53.—A series of trills is sometimes played without the turn, except at the last, thus :—

Ex. 145.

Written.   Performed.   *Turn.*

When the trill is very long, and the fingers tire, they may sometimes be changed; but as this deranges the position of the hand, it must be very carefully managed, or a jerky, hitchy performance will be the result.

["Pupils should *learn* to change fingers on trills, *e. g.*, 1 3 2 4 3 5 3 4 2 3 1, or 1 3 2 4 1 3 2 4, or 2 4 3 4; and for all such practice, as well as for general trill-practice, a triplet accent is of great value, in securing mental and will-power in connection with equality of touch, thus, 𝄞♩♩ ♩♩♩ ♩♩♩ ♩♩♩, etc."—W. H. S]

The trills in thirds, fourths and sixths, can best be explained by the teacher as they occur. The trill is an important ornament in piano-playing; it requires long and unremitting study to bring it to perfection. The student is often tempted to practice too rapidly; but it should be kept continually in mind, that to acquire a full and perfect trill, it must be practiced *very slowly*, and by *raising the fingers a great deal*. The slow trill should be practiced with every variety of shading, from *ff* to *pp*. Great care should be taken to connect well the last two tones of the turn, and play them with ease and smoothness.

325. *What is a* MORDENTE? (See Remark 4, p. 62.)

The Mordente is a short trill, consisting of only two tones, viz., the principal tone and the tone above it, and is made without the turn.

EX. 146. THE MORDENTE.

Written.   Performed.

326. *What duration is given to an Appoggiatura?*

It usually receives one-half of the time of the note before which it is placed.

EX. 147. THE APPOGGIATURA.

Written.   Performed.

327. *When the Appoggiatura occurs before a dotted note, what is its time-value?*

It should still receive half the time-value of the principal note, regardless of the dot.

EX. 148. THE APPOGGIATURA BEFORE A DOTTED NOTE

Written.   Performed.

328. *When an appoggiatura is placed before a note in a chord, how should it be played?*

As the appoggiatura takes the time of part of its principal, the other members of the chord must be struck with the appoggiatura, the principal being played afterward.

Ex. 149. The Appoggiatura before a Chord.

Written. Performed. Written. Performed.

329. *When appoggiaturas occur before all the notes of a chord, how are they to be played?* (See Remark 5, p. 62.)

The appoggiaturas enter with the base, the chord afterward.

Ex. 150. The Chord Appoggiatura.

Written.   Performed.

330. *How is the Acciaccatura represented?*

By an eighth note, or a sixteenth note, with a line dashed obliquely across the stem and hook.

Ex. 151. The Acciaccatura.

331. *How does the acciaccatura differ from the appoggiatura?*

The acciaccatura has no appreciable time-value. As its name indicates (*crush*), it is crushed against the principal tone, usually from the interval of a minor second, and is always accented.

Note 54—"I have seen notes intended as you explain the Acciaccatura, written in thirds, octaves and tenths, etc., *e. g.*, from Chopin's first waltz."—W. H. S.

Ex. 152.

332. *How are small notes played which are more than one degree from the principal note?*

They are always to be played very short, as are also all groups of small notes.

Ex. 153. Groups of Small Notes, etc.

Written.   Performed.

333. *What is a triplet?*

Three equal tones performed in the time of one pulse; the time usually given to two tones divided into three equal parts.

334. *How are triplets represented?*

By three notes grouped with a slur or tie, and marked with a figure 3.

Ex. 154. TRIPLETS.

335. *What is a sextolet?*

Six equal tones performed in the time of one pulse; the time usually given to four tones divided into six equal parts.

336. *How are sextolets represented?*

By six notes grouped with a slur or tie, and marked with a figure 6.

Ex. 155. SEXTOLETS.

NOTE 55.—Five notes are frequently to be performed in the time of one pulse, marked 5; seven to one pulse, marked 7; and many other irregular combinations, such as 9, 11, 13, etc.

Almost every student finds great difficulty in playing a group of two notes with one hand, against a group of three with the other hand, or four with six, six with eight, or eight with twelve; the effect in all these cases is liable to be jerky, spasmodic and limping, and can only be overcome by practicing them very slowly, thus taking time to examine and analyze them with extreme care and deliberation. The following example from Beethoven will show the mode of proceeding :—

Ex. 156.

Divide the triplets into six counts: play both hands on *one*, right hand on *three*, left hand on *four*, and right hand on *five*.

NOTE 56.—"This *slow* method is scientifically correct. However, it does not teach all that is needed; a velocity exercise with a settled, regular unit of counting, where the hands play with a rush, first separately, then together, is often indispensable. For examples involving difficulties of this nature, see Kullak's Edition of Chopin's

Etudes, Op. 25, No. 2; also F minor and A flat major Etudes (posthumous). The following is from the first movement of Beethoven's Sonata, Op. 14, No. 2, in G:—

Ex. 157.

Count four without deviation in rapidity, playing the first four measures many times without stopping, then dashing immediately into the following measures without any attempt at analysis."—W. H. S.

REMARK 3.—"To get at the relations of two to three, three to four and four to five in slow practice, the subjoined diagrams are useful:—

TWO TO THREE.

THREE TO FOUR.

FOUR TO FIVE.

Alternately with this method, practice as shown in Note 53."—A. R. P.

REMARK 4.—"The *Mordente* (No. 325, page 59) was represented in olden times by the sign ⌁, and the *inverted mordente* by the sign ⌁. In modern music the latter only is used. It is identical with the German '*Pralltriller*,' see 'Ten Real Embellishments' (pages 19–21), by E. D. Wagner, translated by C. L. Doll, pub. by E. Schuberth, N. Y. See also 'Die Ornamentik der Klassischen Klavier-Musik' (pages 8–10), by Ludwig Klee, pub. by Breitkopf & Hartel, Leipzig."—Wm. M.

REMARK 5.—*Page 60, No. 329.* "This rule will not always work, as will be seen if strictly applied to Chopin's Nocturne in G minor, Op. 37, No. 1. It is, however, generally correct; see 'Rieman's Musik-Lexicon,' Leipzig, 1882, page 963, under the article 'Verzierungen.'"—Wm. M.

337. *What are runs?*

Groups of regular and irregular numbers of notes (sometimes written in small notes), usually to be played very rapidly.

Ex. 158.   A RUN.

CHAPTER XII.

ABBREVIATIONS; THE C CLEF, Etc.

338. *What is the meaning of a dash over a whole note, or through the stem of a half note or a quarter note?*

It shows that the note so marked must be divided into eighth notes.

Ex. 159.

Written.

Performed.

339. *What is the meaning of a double dash through the stem of a half note or a quarter note?*

It shows that the note so marked must be divided into sixteenth notes.

Ex. 160.

Written.

Performed.

340. *What is the meaning of a dash following a group of notes?*

It shows that the group is to be repeated; it is used merely to obviate the necessity of writing or printing the passage in full.

Ex. 161.

Written.

Performed.

341. *How are whole-measure rests abbreviated?*

A whole rest fills a measure, whatever the time-value of the measure may be; when thus used, it is called a *whole-measure rest* :—

EX. 162. WHOLE-MEASURE RESTS.

342. *How is a two-measure rest indicated?*

A two-measure rest is indicated by a block drawn vertically from the third line to the fourth line of the staff, and sometimes marked with the figure 2, thus :—

EX. 163. TWO-MEASURE RESTS.

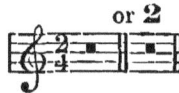

or **2**

343. *How is a four-measure rest indicated?*

A four-measure rest is indicated by a block drawn vertically from the second line to the fourth line of the staff, and sometimes marked with the figure 4, thus :—

EX. 164. A FOUR-MEASURE REST.

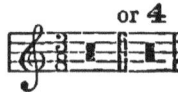

or **4**

344. *When a greater number of measures are to be counted in silence, how are they indicated?*

Simply by figures, or sometimes by a broad dash, or two broad dashes drawn obliquely across the staff, with the figures indicating the number of measures, thus :—

EX. 165. VARIOUS MEASURE RESTS.

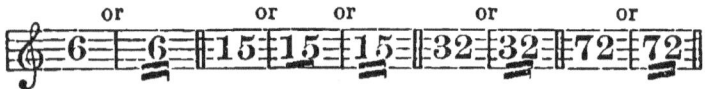

or   or   or   or   or

6   6   15   15   15   32   32   72   72

345. *How are such measure rests counted?*

By naming the number of the measure on the first count in the measure.

NOTE 57.—Thus these seven-measure rests would be counted as follows:—

EX. 166.

7

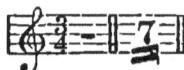

1, 2, 3, | **2,** 2, 3, | **3,** 2, 3, | **4,** 2, 3, | **5,** 2, 3, | **6,** 2, 3, | **7,** 2, 3.

846. *When half notes are tied with a dash across the ends of their stems, how are they to be performed?*

They are to be considered as eighth notes, and struck alternately as many times as would equal the value of a half note.

Ex. 167.

Written.

Performed.

347. *When half notes are connected by two dashes, how are they to be played?*

They are to be considered as sixteenth notes, and struck alternately as many times as would equal the value of a half note.

Ex. 168.

Written

Performed.

348. *When half notes are connected by three dashes, how are they to be played?*

They are to be considered as thirty-second notes, and struck alternately as many times as would equal the value of a half note.

Ex. 169.

Donizetti.

NOTE. 58.—The above example is to be played as if written as follows:—

Ex. 170.

NOTE 59.—If the word *tremulando*, or *tremando*, or *trem.*, be added, they are to be played as quickly as possible, like a *trill*.

349. *When the word* ARPEGGIO *is placed over chords, how are they to be played?*

The tones of such chords are to be played successively from the lowest to the highest. (See Chapter XXIII.)

Ex. 171.

Written.   Performed.

NOTE 60.—"Arpeggio" placed over chords has, in Bach and Handel, a more extended meaning. It frequently takes in both hands, *both up and down*, thus:—

Ex. 172.

Written.   Performed.

See Von Bülow, Tausig and Liszt editions of the various works of Bach and Händel.—C. F.

350. *What is the meaning of 8va.........?*

It is the abbreviation of the word *Ottava*, usually meaning *Ottava alta* (an octave higher), and signifies that the notes over which it is placed should be played an octave higher. It is used in very high passages for the purpose of avoiding the necessity of a bewildering number of added lines. *8va Bassa* (an octave lower) is frequently used.

351. *How is the 8va counteracted?*

By the word *loco*, which denotes a return to the apparent position on the staff, or by a sharp angle in the continuing line, or both, thus:—

Written.

Performed.

NOTE 61.—Sometimes the words *con ottavi*, or *con 8vi*, are used, which mean that the passage is to be played in octaves; if written over the passage, the octave above must be added; if written under the passage, the octave below must be added, thus:—

Ex. 175.

con 8ve...........................

Written.   Performed.

352. *In piano and organ music, how many staffs are usually included by a Brace?*

Two; the Treble staff and the Bass staff.

353. *The upper staff is generally for which hand?*

The right hand.

354. *The lower staff is generally for which hand?*

The left hand.

355. *Are there any exceptions to these rules?*

There are; the right hand occasionally plays from the lower staff, and the left hand from the upper staff.

356. *How are such exceptions indicated?*

By the letters R. H. or M. D., when the right hand is to play from the lower staff, crossing over the left; and L. H. or M. G., when the left hand is to play from the upper staff, crossing over the right.

NOTE 62.—The letters M. D. are the initials of the French words *Main* (hand), and *Droite* (right); M. G. mean *Main* (hand), and *Gauche* (left). The Italian M. D. (*Mano Destra*), and M. S. (*Mano Sinistra*), are often met with.

357. *Are the clefs ever transferred from one staff to the other?*

Very frequently. The Bass clef is temporarily placed upon the upper staff when very low tones are to be played with the right hand, and the Treble clef is temporarily placed upon the lower staff when very high tones are to be played with the left hand.

358. *Is there any other clef besides the Bass and Treble clefs?*

A clef called the C clef is used in instrumental scores (for orchestras), and was formerly much used in vocal music, but never in piano music.

359. *What tone does it always represent?*

Middle C.

360. *What were its several positions on the staff?*

It was placed on the first line as a Soprano clef; on the second line as a Mezzo-Soprano clef; on the third line as an Alto clef; and on the fourth line as a Tenor clef.

EX. 176. THE C CLEF IN ITS SEVERAL POSITIONS.

Soprano Clef.   Same as this.

C D E F G A B C   C D E F G A B C

Ex. 177.

Mezzo-Soprano Clef.   Same as this.

C D E F G A B C   C D E F G A B C

Ex. 178.

Alto Clef.   Same as this.

C D E F G A B C   C D E F G A B C

Ex. 179.

Tenor Clef.   Same as this.

C D E F G A B C   C D E F G A B C

NOTE 63.—The C clef, as described above, is rarely used by modern composers, and is explained here more as a curious relic of bygone times than as a material aid to the learner. Most of the music which was written with this clef in its several positions, has been reprinted in our modern notation (except in orchestral music, in which these clefs are used for certain instruments).

There has been adopted in America, however, within the past fifteen years, a C clef, which is very sensible, indeed, one which simply tells the truth without increasing the difficulty in learning to read music. This C clef fixes *middle C* on the *third space* of the staff, and is used for the Tenor in vocal music; it does not change the pitch-names of the lines and spaces of the staff, but gives the exact pitches which the Tenor voice sings, thus:—

Ex. 180.   THE C CLEF AS A MODERN TENOR CLEF.

361. *What notes and rests were formerly used, other than those given in Chapter I?*

The LONG, which is four times the duration of our whole note, with its corresponding rest, thus:—

Ex. 181.   THE LONG AND REST.*

NOTE 64.—The LONG, however, is seldom seen at present, except in old English church music.

We also sometimes find the one hundred and twenty-eighth note, which is one-half as long as a sixty-fourth note. (See Beethoven's Sonata Pathetique.)

Ex. 182.   THE ONE HUNDRED AND TWENTY-EIGHTH NOTE AND REST.

* REMARK 6 —Dr. Mason says: "It seems to me that, if you refer at all to these old and obsolete notes, the explanation should be more comprehensive, viz.:—
  a. MAXIMA equals eight whole notes.
  b. LONGA   "   four   "   "
  c. BREVIS   "   two   "   "

NOTES.				RESTS.		
Maxima.	Longa.	Brevis.		Maxima.	Longa.	Brevis.

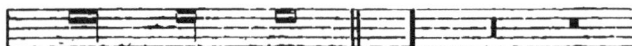

CHAPTER XIII.

THE TIE, SLUR, SYNCOPATION, Etc.

362. *For what is the* DIRECT (∿) *used?*

It was formerly placed at the end of a staff, or at the bottom of a page, to indicate to the performer the position of the next note.

NOTE 65.—The DIRECT will frequently be found in modern English organ accompaniments, when written in pure four-part harmony. It has there, however, a somewhat different meaning, being used only when two parts, one of which is in each hand, come upon the same note. In this case the note is written for the hand which most easily plays it, the other hand having the mark on the proper line or space, to show what the "*voice-leading*" is, thus:—

Ex. 183. THE DIRECT IN ORGAN MUSIC.

363. *What is a* TIE *or* BIND?

A curved line drawn over or under two notes on the same degree of the staff.

364. *How are such notes to be played?*

The key is to be struck with the first note only, but held down the full length of both.

Ex. 184. THE TIE OR BIND.

Written.

Ex. 185.

Performed.

365. *What is a* SLUR *?*

A Slur is a curved line drawn over two or more notes on different degrees of the staff, to denote that they are to be played in a smooth and connected manner.

366. *When two notes are marked with a slur, how are they to be played?*

The first should be struck firmly; the second should be softer and short. (See Remark 7, p. 72.)

Ex. 186.

Written. Performed. Written. Performed.

367. *What is meant by* SYNCOPATION *?*

The commencing of a tone on an unaccented pulse of a measure, and continuing it into the following accented pulse, thereby temporarily displacing the usual accent.

368. *What is such displaced accent called?*

Emphasis.

NOTE 66.—While this use of the word emphasis is not universally employed, it is rapidly gaining favor with musicians, for whenever syncopation takes place, it calls for extra force on the tones which are usually unaccented, and there should be some distinctive term by which such extra force is distinguished from accent. Inasmuch as this extra force predominates to the utter exclusion of the usual accent, thereby proving its superiority for the time being, the term *emphasis* is particularly appropriate, for "the province of *emphasis* is so much more important than *accent*, that the customary seat of the latter is changed when the claims of emphasis require it." (See under "emphasis," in Webster's Dictionary.)

369. *How is Syncopation usually expressed?*

By a long note between two shorter ones (*a*); by an unaccented note tied to an accented one (*b*); and by a note beginning on the last half of one pulse and continuing through the first half of the next (*c*).

Ex. 187.

(*a*) (*b*) (*c*)

370. *How is the emphasis usually marked?*

By two suddenly converging lines (>), or by the word *sforzando* or its abbreviation *sf*, or *fz*, or *sfz*.

371. *In a syncopated passage, how can the player keep the time?*

The Bass and Treble rarely syncopate together; one usually marks the regular time by equal notes.

NOTE 67.—In modern music, long passages are of frequent occurrence, in which both hands syncopate at once. Schumann was one of the first to use this effect extensively; since his time it has become very common.—C.F. (See Remark 8, p. 75.)

372. Is emphasis ever employed in the usual divisions of a measure?

Very frequently; when certain effects are desired, the composer directs the emphasis to be given to what is usually the weak part of the measure, thus :—

Ex. 188.

373. What are the technical names of the several numbers of a key?

8 is called Tonic.

7 is called Sub-Tonic (or Leading Tone).

6 is called Sub-Mediant.

5 is called Dominant.

4 is called Sub-Dominant.

3 is called Mediant.

2 is called Super-Tonic.

1 is called Tonic (or Key-tone).

374. Are these names applied to the minor keys as well as to the major keys?

They are.

Remark 7.—*Page 71, No. 366.*—This answer does not cover the whole ground. If the first of the two notes falls on an *unaccented* part of the measure, *it should not be accented.* Dr. Mason says : "A slur has nothing to do with the accent. The accented part of the measure should always be accented, unless the composer expressly directs otherwise. Passages like Ex. 186 are perhaps more common than the reverse, and this fact may account for the origin of the rule, which I, nevertheless, think is illogical. The example (186) is correct, but so is the following :—

I think the office of the slur is solely and simply *to bind.*"

CHAPTER XIV.

MOVEMENT AND EXPRESSION.

375. *How is the movement of a piece of music determined?*

The most accurate way of showing how fast or slow a piece of music should be performed, is by the use of Maelzel's Metronome. (See page 52 for a description of the Metronome.) There are also certain technical terms taken from the Italian language, which are used for the same purpose by musicians of all languages.

NOTE 68.—Some German musicians, with Schumann at their head, have refused to fall into the general custom, and put nearly all their directions in their own language. Certain English and American church writers have feebly attempted to follow this unwise custom; unwise, because it would necessitate the learning of all languages by every broad-minded musician.—C. F

NOTE 69.—In the following table the terms, which refer to the movement or *tempo*, have been graded, so as to form a scale of degrees from slow to fast. If composers would agree upon some such order of gradation, we would be able to determine the movement of a piece of music with greater accuracy.

FIRST CLASS.—From 50 to 60 beats per minute.
{ *Adagio.* *Grave.* *Lento.* *Largo.* }
Very slow.

SECOND CLASS.—From 56 to 76 beats per minute.
{ *Larghetto.* *Andante.* *Andantino.* *Moderato.* }
Gentle and distinct; somewhat less slow than the first class.

THIRD CLASS.—From 72 to 104 beats per minute.
{ *Maestoso.* *Allegretto.* *Tempo giusto.* *Con commodo.* }
This is the middle class, and indicates a brisk, but serious and dignified movement.

FOURTH CLASS.—From 100 to 132 beats per minute.
{ *Allegro.* *Vivace.* *Con spirito.* *Spiritoso.* }
Brilliant and spirited.

FIFTH CLASS.—From 126 to 160 beats per minute. { *Con brio.* *Con fuoco.* *Presto.* *Prestissimo.* } This class indicates the utmost degree of rapidity.

These are the principal words which are used for the purpose of indicating movement; their meaning, however, is frequently modified and intensified by the use of other words, such as the following:—

Assai, very; as, *Adagio assai,* very slow; *Allegro assai,* very brisk, very lively; *Moderato assai,* very moderately.

Meno, less; as *Meno adagio,* less slow; *Meno allegro,* less fast; *Meno mossa,* less motion.

Molto, much, greatly; as *Molto allegro,* much more lively; *Molto adagio,* much more slowly. This word is more frequently used for the purpose of modifying terms which indicate expression and style. *Molto crescendo,* increase greatly; *Molto diminuendo,* decrease greatly.

Mossa, motion (this word is almost universally written *mosso,* which is a participle, and means changed, moved, affected).

Piu, more; as *Piu adagio,* more slowly; *Piu allegro,* more lively; *Piu mossa,* more motion (faster).

Poco, a little, slightly, somewhat; as *Poco adagio,* somewhat slow; *Poco lento,* a little slow. *Poco* is the opposite of *Molto.* The signification of *Meno* (less) and *Piu* (more), is often modified by *Poco,* as *Poco piu mossa,* a little more motion; *Poco piu presto,* a little more rapidly.

Quasi, as, like, almost; as *Largo quasi andante,* in a broad, large style, but somewhat less slowly; almost *andante.*

Troppo, too much; as a musical term it is generally used with *Non* (not) and *Ma* (but), as *Ma non troppo,* but not too much, *e. g.,* *Adagio ma non troppo,* slow, but not too much so; *Allegro ma non troppo,* fast, but not too much so.

Tempo, time; as *Tempo primo,* in the original time.

376. *How are the style and expression of a piece of music indicated?*

By certain words from the Italian language, which, like those indicating movement, are understood and employed by musicians of all languages.

NOTE 70.—The following list includes the principal terms which are used for the purpose of indicating the style and expression of musical compositions. As the correct pronunciations are given in the "Glossary of Musical Terms" at the close of the present volume, they are omitted here.

Ad libitum. At pleasure.
Accelerando. Faster and faster.
Affettuoso. Affectionately; tenderly; with feeling.
Afflizione. Sorrowfully.
Agitato. With agitation.
Amabile. Amiably.
Animato. With animation.
Brilliante. Brilliantly; sparklingly.
Calando. Retarding and decreasing.
Cantabile. In a graceful, singing style.
Crescendo. Gradually increasing in strength or power.
Con precisione. With precision.
Dolce. Sweetly; softly.
Doloroso. Painfully; sorrowfully.
Diminuendo. Gradually diminishing.
Delicato. Delicately.
Forte. Loud; fourth degree of power.
Fortissimo. Very loud; fifth degree of power.

Furioso. Furiously.
Grazioso. Gracefully; with elegance.
Indiciso. Undecided.
Innocente. Artless; unassuming.
Marcato. Marked; prominent.
Mezzo. Half way; middling; the third degree of power.
Morendo. Gradually decreasing.
Piano. Soft; the second degree of power.
Pianissimo. Very soft; the first degree of power.
Placido. Placid; pleasant; gentle.
Ritardando. Slackening the time.
Scherzando. Playfully; sportively.
Simplice. Simple; chaste.
Sforzando. With emphasis on one particular tone.
Sostenuto. Sustained and smooth.
Staccato. Short and distinct; detached.
Tranquillo. Tranquilly.
Tremando. Tremblingly.

REMARK 8.—*Page 71, Note 67.* "Is this statement scientifically accurate? Syncopation cannot extend over long passages without losing its characteristic nature. The regular and normal pulsations must be made manifest at comparatively short intervals or true syncopation ceases. There cannot be contrast without *antithesis* or opposition. The long passages referred to in Schumann's works, which seem to the *eye* as syncopation, are in reality an augmentation, enlargement or broadening of the time. Notice that the following passage from Schumann's *Concerto in A minor*, is in ¾ measure:—

SCHUMANN'S ORIGINAL NOTATION.

etc.

This is a syncopation to the eye, but to the ear the effect is practically as in the following example, which certainly greatly simplifies the passage:—

ALTERED NOTATION (for illustration).

etc.

The foregoing example is from a work entitled "Pianistic Expression" (Das Verständniss im Clavierspiel), in which this subject has received able treatment. It is by A. F. Christiani. Published by Harper & Brothers, N. Y.—Wm. M.

CHAPTER XV.

THE KEY-BOARD.

377. *How is the key-board of a piano-forte or organ divided?*

Into white keys and black keys.

378. *What are the black keys called?*

Sharps and flats.

379. *How are the black keys further divided?*

Into alternate groups of two and three.

EX. 189. BLACK KEY GROUPS.

Group of two.	Group of three.	Group of two.	Group of three.

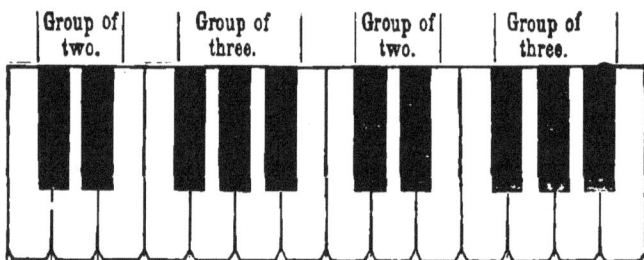

680. *How are the white keys named?*

From the names of the first seven letters of the alphabet: A, B, C, D, E, F and G.

381. *How are these names applied to the key-board?*

The white key at the left of the *duo-group* is C; the white key at the right of the *duo-group* is E; the white key between the two is D; the white key at the left of the *tri-group* is F; the white key at the right of the *tri-group* is B; the two white keys between F and B (or *in the tri-group*) are G and A.

Ex. 190. NAMES OF THE WHITE KEYS.

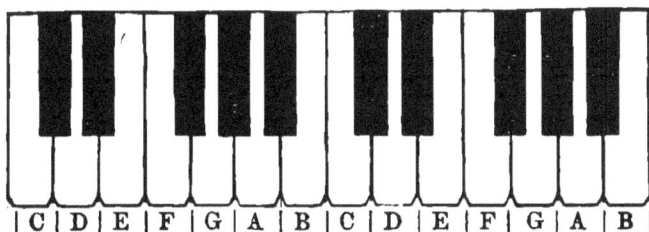

| C | D | E | F | G | A | B | C | D | E | F | G | A | B |

382. *How are the black keys named?*

Each black key takes its name from the white key on either side.

383. *If we read from left to right (low to high) what will the black keys be called?*

Sharps.

384. *If we read from right to left (high to low) what will the black keys be called?*

Flats.

385. *What is the name of the black key between C and D?*

C sharp or D flat.

386. *What is the name of the black key between D and E?*

D sharp or E flat.

387. *What is the name of the black key between F and G?*

F sharp or G flat.

388. *What is the name of the black key between G and A?*

G sharp or A flat.

389. *What is the name of the black key between A and B?*

A sharp or B flat.

Ex. 191. NAMES OF BLACK KEYS.

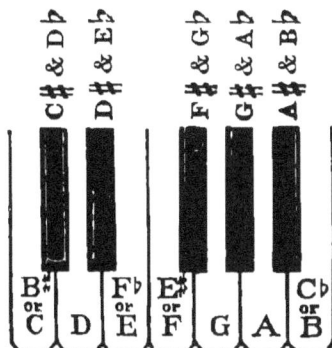

390. *Which is middle C?*

The C which is about midway between the two ends of the key-board.

Ex. 192. THE KEY-BOARD, SHOWING MIDDLE C.

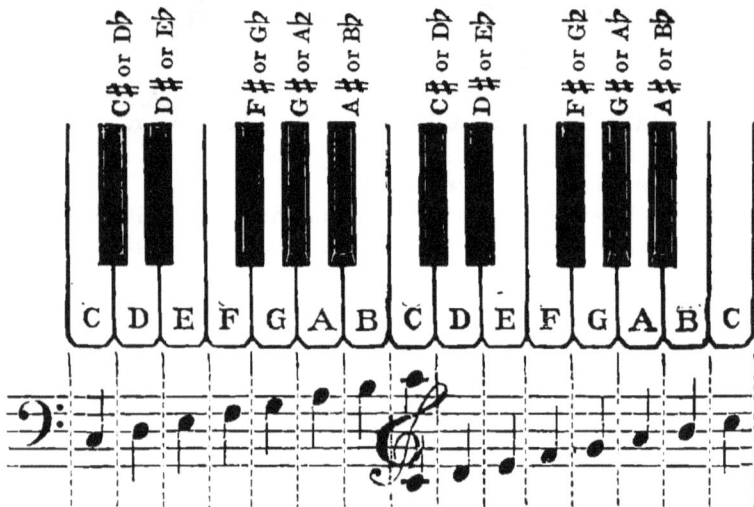

391. *What comprises an octave on the key-board?*

An octave comprises all the keys (black and white) from any given key to the next one of the same name, either up or down.

392. *How many groups of black keys are there in each octave?*

Two; a duo-group and a tri-group.

393. *Of how many octaves of keys does a piano-forte key-board consist?*

Most modern pianos are made with seven octaves of keys.

NOTE 71.—On the opposite page will be found a representation of the key-board of a seven-octave piano, together with its corresponding notes on the staff.

394. *What is an* ENHARMONIC CHANGE?

The changing of the name and representation of a tone without changing its pitch.

NOTE 72.—The ancients used a scale which progressed by intervals that were one-half as great as our half-step, and called it the Enharmonic Scale. This scale became obsolete long ago, and the word "Enharmonic" is now never used except to indicate a change of name, representation and resolution (tendency), without change of pitch.

395. *Is every tone capable of an Enharmonic Change?*

All tones can be thus changed.

KEY-BOARD AND SCALE OF A SEVEN AND ONE-THIRD OCTAVE PIANO-FORTE.

396. C changed enharmonically becomes what ?
B♯, or D double flat.

Ex. 193. THE PITCH C, ENHARMONICALLY CHANGED.

397. C♯ changed enharmonically becomes what ?
D♭.

Ex. 194. THE PITCH C♯, ENHARMONICALLY CHANGED.

898. D changed enharmonically becomes what ?
C double sharp, or E double flat.

Ex. 195. THE PITCH D, ENHARMONICALLY CHANGED.

399. D♯ changed enharmonically becomes what?
E♭.

Ex. 196. THE PITCH D♯, ENHARMONICALLY CHANGED.

400. E changed enharmonically becomes what?
D double sharp, or F♭.

Ex. 197. THE PITCH E, ENHARMONICALLY CHANGED.

401. F changed enharmonically becomes what?
E♯, or G double flat.

Ex. 198. THE PITCH F, ENHARMONICALLY CHANGED.

402. F♯ changed enharmonically becomes what?
G♭.

Ex. 199. THE PITCH F♯, ENHARMONICALLY CHANGED.

403. G changed enharmonically becomes what ?
F double sharp, or A double flat.

Ex. 200. The Pitch G, Enharmonically Changed.

404. *G♯ changed enharmonically becomes what ?*
A♭.

Ex. 201. The Pitch G♯, Enharmonically Changed.

405. *A changed enharmonically becomes what ?*
G double sharp, or B double flat.

Ex. 202. The Pitch A, Enharmonically Changed.

406. *A♯ changed enharmonically becomes what ?*
B♭.

Ex. 203. The Pitch A♯, Enharmonically Changed.

407. *B changed enharmonically becomes what ?*
A double sharp, or C♭.

Ex. 204. The Pitch B, Enharmonically Changed.

408. *On what key is C♯ played?*
On the black key between C and D.
409. *On what key is D♯ played?*
On the black key between D and E.
410. *On what key is E♯ played?*
On the white key F.
411. *On what key is F♯ played?*
On the black key between F and G.
412. *On what key is G♯ played?*
On the black key between G and A.
413. *On what key is A♯ played?*
On the black key between A and B.
414. *On what key is B♯ played?*
On the white key C.
415. *On what key is C♭ played?*
On the white key B.

416. *On what key is Bb played?*

On the black key between B and A.

417. *On what key is Ab played?*

On the black key between A and G.

418. *On what key is Gb played?*

On the black key between G and F.

419. *On what key is Fb played?*

On the white key E.

420. *On what key is Eb played?*

On the black key between E and D.

421. *On what key is Db played?*

On the black key between D and C.

422. *On what key is C double sharp played?*

On the white key D.

423. *On what key is D double sharp played?*

On the white key E.

424. *On what key is F double sharp played?*

On the white key G.

425. *On what key is G double sharp played?*

On the white key A.

426. *On what key is A double sharp played?*

On the white key B.

427. *Why are E double sharp and B double sharp never used?*

Because they belong to scales which are so remote as to be of no practical use.

428. *On what key is B double flat played?*

On the white key A.

429. *On what key is A double flat played?*

On the white key G.

430. *On what key is G double flat played?*

On the white key F.

431. *On what key is E double flat played?*

On the white key D.

432. *On what key is D double flat played?*

On the white key C.

433. *Why are C double flat and F double flat never used?*

Because they are of no practical use.

NOTE 73.—Scales so remote as to require double sharps or double flats in the signature are rarely used, except for those who aim at great proficiency in reading music, and even in such cases it is doubtful whether the same degree of proficiency cannot be gained in other ways.

NOTE 74.—On the opposite page will be found illustrated the enharmonic capabilities of the key-board.

THE KEY-BOARD ENHARMONICALLY CONSIDERED

Ex. 205.

Key	Sharps	Flats
C	B♯	D♭♭
D	C♯♯	E♭♭
E	D♯♯	F♭
F	E♯	G♭♭
G	F♯♯	A♭♭
A	G♯♯	B♭♭
B	A♯♯	C♭
C	B♯	D♭♭

C♯ D♭   D♯ E♭   F♯ G♭   G♯ A♭   A♯ B♭

Ex. 206. Absolute Pitch-Names of Tones in the Italian and German Languages, as Compared with those in the English Language.

German Names.

cis or des.	dis or es.	fis or ges.	gis or as.	ais.	B.	C.	Enharmonic Sharps and Flats.
C.	D.	E.	F.	G.	A.	H.	C.	Absolute Pitch Names.

Italian Names.

sin or rerr.	donn or mirr.	renn or larr.	min or sorr.	fann or farr.	sonn or sorr.	lann or dor.	sin or rerr.	Enharmonic Double Sharps and Double Flats.
don or rerr.	ren or mir.	fan or sir.	sor or lar.	lan or sir.		don or rerr.		Enharmonic Sharps and Flats.
Do.	Re.	Mi.	Fa.	Sol.	La.	Si.	Do.	Absolute Pitch Names.

American and English Names.

B♯ or D♭♭	C♯ or E♭♭	D♯ or F♭♭	E♯ or G♭♭	F♯ or A♭♭	G♯ or B♭♭	A♯ or C♭♭	B♯ or D♭♭	Enharmonic Double Sharps and Double Flats.
C♯ or D♭	D♯ or E♭		F♯ or G♭	G♯ or A♭	A♯ or B♭		C♯ or D♭	Enharmonic Sharps and Flats.
C.	D.	E.	F.	G.	A.	B.	C.	Absolute Pitch Names.

Note 75.—It will be noticed that in Germany the white keys have the same names as in America, except B, which they call H (hah); the sharps take their names from the letters, adding *is*, thus C♯ is cis (cease), D♯ is dis (deece), F♯ is fis (feece), G♯ is gis (geese), etc.; the flats follow a similar order, except B♭, which they call B (bay), A♭ is as (ahs), G♭ is ges (gace), E♭ is es (ace), and D♭ is des (dace).

In Italy the syllables Do, Re, Mi, etc., are used as absolute pitch names (as we use letters); the sharps take *n* after the syllable name, thus, C♯ is don (doan), D♯ is ren (rain), F♯ is fan (fahn), G♯ is son (sown), A♯ is lan (lahn); the flats take *r* after the syllable name, thus, B♭ is sir (seer), A♭ is lar (lahr), G♭ is sor (soar), E♭ is mir (meer), and D♭ is rer (rayr); but most bungling of all is their mode of naming double sharps and double flats, the double sharps taking double *nn*, thus, donn, renn, fann, sonn, lann; and the double flats double *rr*, thus, sirr, larr, sorr, mirr, and rerr.

American musicians have reason to congratulate themselves, not only that they are rid of English crotchets and quavers, and hemi-demi-semi-quavers, and every other similar hemi-demi-semi monstrosity, but that they are also free from Italian and French modes of naming tones, and sol-fa-ing.

CHAPTER XVI.

POSITION OF BODY, ARMS, HANDS, FINGERS, Etc.

434. *What is the correct position at the piano ?*

The player should be seated opposite the middle of the key-board, so that both ends are within convenient reach.

435. *How is the correct distance of the body from the key-board to be ascertained ?*

By placing the hands upon the key-board properly and observing that the elbows are slightly in advance of a perpendicular line drawn from the shoulders.

436. *What should be the height of the seat ?*

The seat should be high enough to bring the elbows on a level with the surface of the keys, or slightly lower.

NOTE 76.—The seat should be *firm*. A strong chair, which is the right height, is far preferable to a revolving stool.

NOTE 77.—The elbows slightly below the level of the keys were better for the following reasons, viz.: it helps make the upper arm more steady; it loosens the wrist by causing a partial separation of the heavy parts of the hand and forearm; it helps the pupil to acquire a *light* wrist, because he must hold it up; a more *limber wrist*, because freer to bend and turn, and it will help toward real individuality of cultivation, distinct articulation and consciousness of the fingers, toward giving better position to both fingers and hand, and toward discriminating better in touch, inasmuch as the pupil with a heavy upper arm, light forearm and wrist, and steady hand, can learn to estimate the weight of the finger in playing independently of force or weight in the arm. It frees one from the bad habits of pushing, bearing down or crowding the fingers. The habits so easily acquired with a high elbow cause the unpracticed pupil to overweight the fingers and touch, thereby frequently injuring the fingers which are already weak, notably the fourth and fifth, causing them to flatten and break down, instead of keeping a firm, arched form. A high elbow generally helps to stiffen the wrist, to elevate the stronger side of the hand, and depress the weaker side, giving undue strength to the thumb, and shortening or cramping the weak fingers. Players thus often mistake the power of a strong arm (which is large and heavy) for that of a small weak finger which the heavy arm causes to play loud. Let us have the finger strength, form, bracing or striking power, independent of the arm. Then we can, for various purposes, safely indulge ourselves occasionally with a high seat. That modern invention of the Yankee, the piano stool, ought to "go." I advise a chair made neither too deep nor shallow, the seat being horizontal (not tipping forward), with a perpendicular back, or one partially suited to the curves of the body. The seat should have no influence on the touch; its back should neither allow of lounging, leaning back lazily, nor crowding forward. The support thereby gained will save much fatigue and energy which were better expended in other directions; it will also keep one from

becoming round-shouldered, or stooping, and in cases of many delicate women and girls, will enable them to avoid ill-health, if not actual disease, frequently induced by unnatural or laborious positions.—W. H. S.

437. *What should be the position of the arms above the elbows?*

They should be kept near to the body, though without touching it.

438. *What should be the position of the feet?*

The ball of the right foot should be placed over the damper pedal, and the ball of the left foot over the soft pedal. (See opposite page.)

NOTE 78.—The damper pedal, commonly called the loud pedal, is used to remove the dampers from the strings, thereby allowing them to continue to vibrate. Great care should be taken to lift the foot from the damper pedal at the instant (sometimes a trifle before) a different chord is struck. Many performers try to conceal their want of skill by a continual use of the damper pedal. Nothing in the whole nature of piano playing is more exasperating to an intelligent listener than an indiscriminate use of this pedal. The soft pedal of an upright or a grand piano usually shifts the key-board and action to one side, causing the hammer to strike one string less, thus softening the tone, *without materially changing the quality* (in some modern pianos this is accomplished by an ingenious device which carries all the hammers nearer to the strings, thereby diminishing the power by lessening the distance). The soft pedal in square pianos merely protrudes a piece of soft buckskin between the hammers and the strings, and for a short time, while the piano is new, answers the purpose indifferently well, but soon becomes worse than useless, for it entirely *changes the quality of the tone.* The keys should never be struck heavily during the use of the soft pedal, as it is liable to injure both the hammer and the tuning of the instrument.

The pedals ought never to be used by beginners nor indeed by any one, until carefully studied with a painstaking and scientific teacher.

NOTE 79.—For children an ottoman or foot stool may be used. Pedals for children have been invented which can be attached to the ordinary pedals.

439. *What are some of the common faults and bad habits which should be strictly guarded against?*

Shrugging the shoulders, swaying the body either backward or forward, or from side to side, protruding the elbows, contortions of the face, such as frowning, raising the eyebrows, and grimacing, crossing the legs, shaking the head, etc. All such habits should be studiously avoided until an easy, graceful and unconstrained position at the piano becomes habitual.

440. *What should be the position of the hand?*

Place the tips of the fingers and the thumb on five successive white keys, exactly over the centre of each key (as regards right and left); keep the wrist at, or slightly above, a level with the hand and arm (neither raised nor lowered, but without constraint); keep the knuckles and knuckle-joints on a level with the back of the hand. The forepart of the fingers should be gently rounded, the last joint of each finger perpendicular to the key.

NOTE 80.—It will be of great service to the student to keep the knuckle-joint of the second finger (index finger) slightly depressed, the knuckle-joints of the fourth and fifth fingers somewhat elevated. This will cause the entire fifth finger to assume a position *nearer* the perpendicular than the others. This touch presumes that the fingers shall rise and fall from the knuckle-joints. This is the most frequently serviceable and the most reliable position for developing strength and certainty of execution.—W. H. S.

NOTE 81.—For light, quick, crisp passages, the knuckle-joints can be held down still firmer, with the fingers more curved, so as to strike nearly on the nails, raising only a short distance and playing almost staccato.—W. H. S.

NOTE 82.—For a more liquid, mellow quality of singing tone, allow the knuckle-joints to rise more, and the fingers to stretch out partially flat: lifting them higher than usual will aid one to produce a fuller, deeper singing quality.—W.H.S.

NOTE 83.—The nails should be kept neatly trimmed, and never allowed to become so long as to touch the keys when the fingers are at the proper curve.

EX. 208. THE CORRECT POSITION OF THE HAND AND FINGERS.

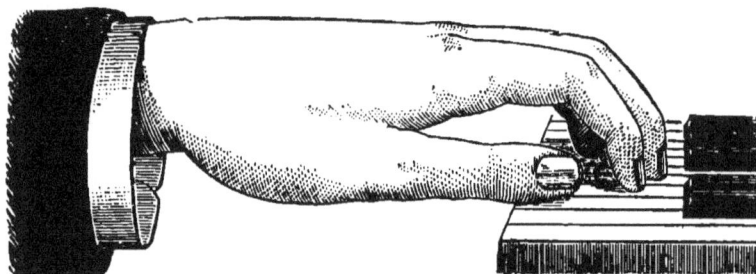

441. *Should the fifth finger be rounded as much as the others ?*
The fourth and fifth fingers should be slightly more extended than the others, and not quite so much rounded. (See Remark 9, p. 89)

EX. 209. THE POSITION AND ACTION OF THE THUMB.

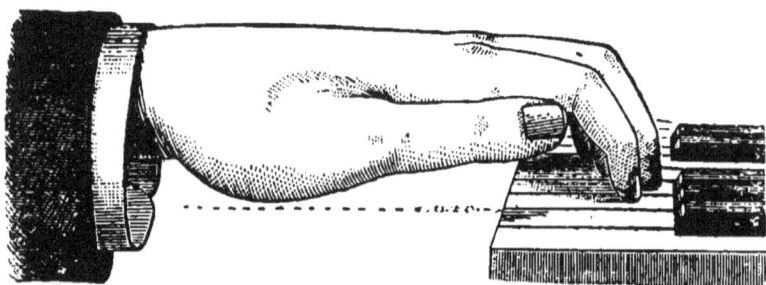

442. *What are the correct position and action of the thumb ?*
The normal position of the thumb should be stretched horizontally so that its outer surface (with which the key is struck) will be on a level with the surface of the key-board; it should be moved by the joint which connects it with the hand, but should never create any motion of the hand itself; it should be kept continually above the keys,

never permitted to hang down in front of them, and should never rest upon the key-board.

NOTE 84.—The joint of the thumb nearest the hand should, ordinarily, be brought out from under the hand considerably, the end joint of the thumb moderately curved in. The action of striking should be caused by the first-named joint rising and falling, not by turning or sticking out the end joint.—W. H. S.

EX. 210. THE POSITION OF THE FOURTH AND FIFTH FINGERS.

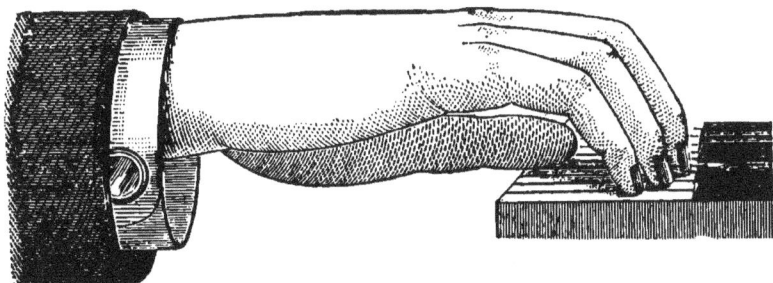

NOTE 85.—The hand, while playing, should be held ordinarily so that the centre of gravity will fall toward the thumb, i. e., the weak side high, the thumb side not high, but also not heavy.

NOTE 86.—The general position of the hand, as also that of the body, should be perfectly easy and natural, a precaution eminently essential to a good style of playing; if the pupil have awkward habits to correct, so that an easy position of body or hand requires great and constant watchfulness, there should be as little appearance of constraint as possible.

REMARK 9.—"The answer to 441 has age, authority, and almost universal citation on its side, but the conditions which so frequently force the fourth and fifth fingers to play in a position 'slightly more extended,'and not quite so much rounded,' are essentially the same in kind as those which occasionally, though less frequently, necessitate the extension of the second and third fingers. As the training of the second and third fingers is not based on these special conditions, but solely with a view to the best development of their powers, so too, the fourth and fifth fingers should assume in technical practice the symmetrical position displayed by the second fingers in Ex. 209, and should cultivate precisely the same movement in all particulars, the only distinction between the second and third fingers and the fourth and fifth being, that the fourth and fifth should practice every motion at least twice as many times as their more advantageously circumstanced comrades."—A. R. P.

CHAPTER XVII.

TOUCH.

443. *What is the main point to be considered as regards the study of touch ?*

The main point of difficulty in the study of *touch* is to learn to connect smoothly two or more successive tones.

444. *Into how many classes may the study of touch be divided, and what are they called ?*

Four : legato touch, legatissimo touch, staccato touch, and portamento touch.

445. *Why is the legato touch most important of all ?*

Because it occurs most frequently and is *always* to be used where no other is especially marked ; it is to be used in all finger exercises with the hand at rest.

NOTE 87.—It is the nature of melody and the song-like element in music. It is the correct touch for running passages requiring execution or brilliancy.—W.H.S.

446. *What are some of the rules for the legato touch ?*

The fingers and thumbs must be moved only from the knuckle-joints ; the unoccupied fingers must be kept at an equal distance from the keys, but not allowed to touch them before the instant of striking ; in striking, the finger must touch the key exactly in the middle ; each finger, after striking a key, must be lifted quickly, and *at the instant when the succeeding finger strikes its key,* so that the successive tones may neither run into each other, nor be separated perceptibly ; no movement of the hand should be permitted other than that which necessarily arises from the moving of the proper muscles and sinews, especially when the other fingers are holding tones ; if a strong, full tone is required, the fingers must be raised so much the higher, and press with greater weight upon the keys ; if the tone is to be subdued, the motion and pressure of the fingers should be more moderate. (See Remark 10, p. 99)

NOTE 88.—In passages which are to be executed with great rapidity, the fingers cannot be raised as high as in slow passages ; however, if rapid passages require great force, or great delicacy, it will be perfectly possible when the strength of the fingers has been developed to the utmost; for, generally, rapid passages may be regarded as a test of a performer's proper cultivation.

447. *How is the* STACCATO TOUCH *executed?*

With the aid of the wrist.

Ex. 211. THE STACCATO TOUCH (striking from the wrist).

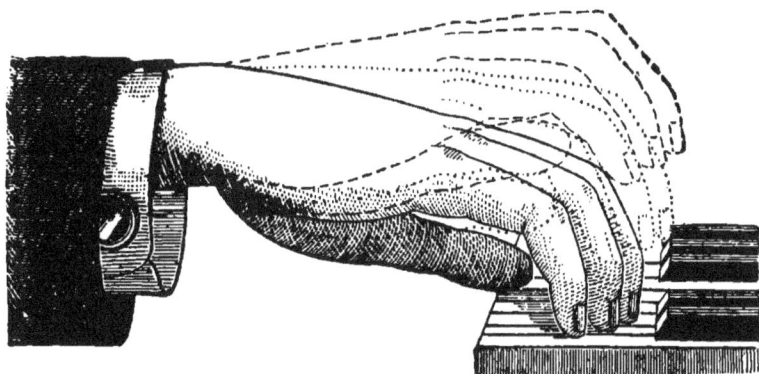

448. *What are some of the rules for the staccato touch?*

The hand must be slightly raised by the wrist, and, with an easy movement, thrown, as it were, upon the keys. As soon as it has struck it must be raised to its former position; the raising of the hand should not be effected by lifting the forearm, which has nothing to do with this movement; in running passages, of course, the arm moves along with the hand.

NOTE 89.—The forearm should be trained to keep perfectly steady in this exercise, neither rising nor falling. Also the fingers should be kept fixed in a curved form, arch-like, never with unnecessary finger movements or hollow places in the knuckles or finger-joints.—W. H. S.

NOTE 90.—Great care, however, should be constantly taken that the arm be not kept too stiff, nor the movement of the hand too violent; otherwise the performer may present a very ludicrous appearance.

In rapid and in soft passages, there is less movement of the wrist than in the medium passages, or in those where force is required; in such rapid or soft passages the staccato may often be produced by merely drawing back the fingers quickly after striking, and without any very marked movement of the wrist.

449. *In what does the legatissimo touch consist?*

It consists in this, that a key, after being struck, is not raised again at the striking of the next one. By this device (which should rarely be employed except with tones that belong to the same harmony) the tones are made to run into each other, as it were, producing a greater fulness of tone.

NOTE 91.—It is a great aid, however, to musical expression when applied to melodies and song-like effects, especially in slow and sonorous themes.—W. H. S.

NOTE 92.—As this mode of touch is to be used only with great care, the student should abstain from it entirely until the legato touch is perfectly mastered. This suffering the fingers to remain upon some keys after others are struck is in direct opposition to the principles of the legato touch, which, unless previously mastered, is thereby rendered so much the more difficult. (See Remark 11, p. 94.)

EX. 212. THE LEGATISSIMO TOUCH.

EX. 213. LEGATO AND LEGATISSIMO COMBINED.

450. *Define the portamento touch.*

The portamento touch may be defined as a compromise between the legato touch and the staccato touch; it is used when notes are marked with dots, over which a slur is drawn (see Ex. 217) or thus: . The tones must be held nearly their full time, and are to be played with a pressure of the fingers corresponding with the strength of tone required, and by slightly raising and dropping the fore-arm.

NOTE 93.—The following examples show the same passage, played first legato, then legatissimo, then staccato, and lastly, portamento.

Ex. 214.

Ex. 215.

Ex. 216.

Ex. 217.

Note 94.—Example 217 should be played as though written somewhat as follows :—

Ex. 218.

Note 95.—Thus far in the present chapter the writer has followed the system of *Touch* as given by Louis Plaidy, Professor of the Piano-Forte at the Conservatorium of Leipzig, but he cannot permit the present opportunity to pass without urging upon all pupils (and more especially the teachers), to make themselves masters of the method of Touch as laid down in Dr. Wm. Mason's "System of Technical Exercises for the Piano-Forte," edited by Mr. W. S. B. Mathews (published by Oliver Ditson & Co.). We are kindly permitted to quote the following synopsis from Dr. Mason's Method of Touch :

TOUCH.

"Touch is divided into *Finger touch, Hand touch, and Arm touch.*

I. Finger Touch.

"This is made by moving the fingers at the third joint, hand and arm being quiet. It consists of two elements, viz. : *The attack* (the force with which the key is struck) : and *the clinging pressure* (whereby the key is held down and the tone prolonged). Legato playing involves both elements; Staccato only the first. There are two forms of *Legato finger touch,* namely : The Clinging Touch and the Plain Legato Touch.

"The Clinging Touch is the extreme form of legato touch. It consists of an *attack* which, at the beginning of a phrase, may come partly from the wrist, but when not beginning a phrase must come from the finger only ; it is prolonged by a *heavy clinging pressure,* the sensation being of pressing down the key. In changing to the next tone this pressure must be transferred to the next key without being assumed by the arm, or at all relaxed. The secret of legato playing is the transference of this *clinging* pressure from one key to the next without partially or entirely relaxing it just before the next key is struck ; such relaxation gives rise to a vertical motion of the hand, a sort of hopping motion, which, when once acquired, is very difficult to overcome.

"In the Plain Legato Touch, the attack, *clinging pressure* and *transference* is the same as in the clinging touch ; it differs from it in that the attack and clinging pressure are not so heavy, and, especially in that the clinging pressure causes a different muscular sensation. In the Clinging Touch the pressure always *exceeds the natural power of the finger, i. e.,* the key is held down intentionally by an effort to do so, while in the Plain Legato Touch the pressure does not exceed the natural force of the finger. The Plain Legato Touch is applicable to all kinds of running passages. The Clinging Touch is applicable to melodies, and is also used in the slow practice of runs.

"Staccato Touch is of two kinds, viz. : The Mild Staccato Touch and the Elastic Touch.

"The Mild Staccato Touch consists of an attack only. It has two forms, namely (*a*), in very rapid passages it is effected by moving the finger from the third joint without sliding the point of the finger on the key ; and (*b*), whenever the time will admit, it is effected by striking the key with the finger moving chiefly on the second joint and sliding inward toward the palm of the hand.

* Sometimes called Mezzo Legato.

"The ELASTIC TOUCH is the *extreme staccato*, and consists of a very forcible attack made by the instantaneous flexion of all the joints of the fingers, *as in the act of spitefully shutting the hand.*

"Among the most troublesome cases with which the teacher will have to deal, are those of pupils who have fallen into the habit of playing everything staccato. The touch they use is neither of those described above, but an objectionable one, made largely with the hand and arm. It may always be recognized by the hopping motion the hand has in playing scales and runs. The fault here is that the *clinging pressure* is either entirely wanting, or is released when the tone is but partially completed." (Here follow instructions and exercises for correcting this fault. See page 22, " Mason's Piano-Forte Technics.")

II. THE HAND TOUCH.

"This is also called the *Wrist Touch*. It is produced by swinging the hand on the wrist joint as a hinge. It is applicable to all staccato chords and octaves, although it may be more or less modified by combination with some one of the finger touches. In the legato octave and chord touch there is a clinging pressure of greater or less force. In staccato octaves there is no clinging pressure. The ELASTIC TOUCH (*extreme staccato*) for chords and octaves is produced chiefly by the fingers, as in the ELASTIC TOUCH already described. (W. H. S. uses a form of fore-arm or hand touch for extreme staccato, especially in heavy chords, or in playing where the time between notes will admit of the greater motion.) The attack-force in heavy passages may be somewhat increased by force from the wrist, and in this touch the natural rebound is greater than the Elastic Touch of the finger only. In its execution, the elbow must not be moved backward or forward. The hand is to be shut spitefully, the fingers striking the keys while in the act of closing, and at the same time, or in consequence of this blow upon the keys, the hand rises slightly from the wrist (which must be held loosely), and presents the appearance of a 'fist.'" (Here follow observations with regard to the artistic application and modification of these different touches. See "Mason's Piano-Forte Technics," page 24.)

III. THE ARM TOUCH.

"This is produced by moving the entire fore-arm and hand on the elbow joint, the fingers and wrist being kept rigid. We mention this touch because it is very often used in playing chords and octaves by those who have not been properly taught. It was the method of octave playing taught as late as the time of Moscheles, but it is now comparatively disused by artists, having been superseded by the *Hand Touch*, which produces a much better tone with less fatigue of muscles." (This last can be taught, *with a pliable wrist*, (I) as a means of accurate phrasing, *e. g.*, as applied to a two-finger exercise : (II) as a means in chords and octaves, of avoiding unnecessary percussion and inaccuracy of the fingers ; (III) as a means of adding weight to a grip-touch, in which the hand does not shut spitefully, but closes only enough to give the fingers a firm grasp of the keys. —W. H. S.) (See Remark 12, below.)

In closing this chapter on Touch, the writer cannot too strongly urge an acquaintance with the work from which these remarks are gleaned. Especial attention is directed to Dr. Mason's "TWO-FINGER EXERCISES;" his "APPLICATION OF RHYTHM TO EXERCISES," and his "SCALES IN CANON FORM," etc., all of which not only tend to greatly lessen the tedium of practice, but, what is much better, they render common practice absolutely interesting.

REMARK 11.—*Page 92, Note 92* "I always begin with the *super-legato* touch and find it works admirably. No danger need be apprehended if another exercise is given to counterbalance and accompany it, and to be practiced alternately in connection with it. Such two exercises are especially admirable in their combined result, as they help each other and, at the same time, each acts as an antidote to correct bad results which might arise from the exclusive practice of either alone."—Wm. M.

REMARK 12. (*On the Arm-Touch.*) "A boy is said to have defined salt as 'some thing that made potato taste *bad when there wasn't any in it.*' So much, at least, may be safely claimed for the ARM-TOUCH in relation to hand and finger-touch in many cases. To leave the fore-arm without systematic training in precision, elasticity and lightness of motion, is to handicap, not aid, the wrist and hand in their own specific work."—A. R. P. [Note the special attention paid to the fore-arm in Mr. Parsons' "Rhythmic Exercises for Fingers, Hand and Fore-arm," New York, G. Schirmer.—H. R. P.]

CHAPTER XVIII,

FINGERING.

451. *What is understood by fingering?*

The proper use of the fingers while playing key-board instruments like the Piano-forte and Organ.

452. *How should the hand be placed?*

The hand should be so placed as to remain as much as possible over five keys, that each finger may cover its respective key, thus rendering the motion of the hand scarcely perceptible.

453. *How is the fingering usually expressed?*

The thumb is marked 1, and the fingers 2, 3, 4 and 5 respectively.*

454. *When a passage requires more than five keys in succession, how is it fingered?*

The thumb must pass under the fingers, and the fingers must pass over the thumb.

455. *Under which fingers may the thumb be passed?*

The thumb may be passed under the second, third and fourth fingers, and, in extreme cases, under the fifth.

Ex. 219.

Right hand.

Ex. 220.

Left hand.

NOTE 96.—When the thumb is to pass under, it should be carried along under the fingers, so as to be under each finger just as that finger strikes its key; thus it will arrive at its own key exactly at the right instant.

NOTE 97.—In rapid scale- and arpeggio-playing, this rule might cause the thumb to arrive at its note too late. A safe rule would be to have the thumb pass one note *beyond* the one to be struck each time; thereby arriving at a point *above* its key an instant *before* it is required. This is a good general rule for all fingers to observe.—W. H. S.

---

* Many excellent teachers, both in England and America, still use ✕, 1, 2, 3, 4; but as, by far, the greater number have adopted 1, 2, 3, 4, 5, it has been thought best to follow that mode of fingering in the present work.

456. *Which fingers may be passed over the thumb ?*

The second, third and fourth fingers may be passed over the thumb, and, in extreme cases, the fifth finger.

Ex. 221.

Right hand.

Ex. 222.

Left hand.

457. *Is it allowable to pass one finger over another ?*

It is not.

Note 98.—These positive rules for fingering are only for those who have not yet developed each and every finger to its utmost capacity, the object being to place the muscles of the hand and fingers under the perfect control of the will, and when this is attained, the student may throw aside these rules, and choose such fingers as are most suitable for executing the passage in the required time and force. Students should not consider themselves free from the law, however, until they have *completely mastered* all these rules for fingering. (See Chapter IX of Dr. Bidez' exhaustive treatise on "The Art of Fingering," an octavo volume of 72 pages devoted to this one subject, and well worth a careful perusal by every teacher. Address Aloys Bidez, L.L. D., Charlotte, North Carolina.)

Note 99.—Both Chopin and Liszt make great use of passing one finger over the other. See Chopin's Etude, Op. 10, No. 3, as an example ; the right hand is fingered thus :—

Ex. 223.

etc.

458. *Is it allowable to play two or three consecutive notes with the same finger ?*

It is not ; every note should be played with a different finger, unless a rest intervenes.

Note 100.—Liszt and Chopin frequently use the same finger for several consecutive notes. See Chopin's Ballade in F minor :—

Ex. 224.

etc.

for an example for the thumb ; and I also call to mind (without being able at this moment to find them) cases where a slow scale has been fingered with the third or fourth finger all the way down, for special effects.—C. F.(See Remark 13, p. 93.)

NOTE 101.—The last two notes are given for the benefit of players who are suffi-ciently advanced to be able to comprehend the necessity for all such exceptions to our general rules. As was remarked in Note 98, "Students should not consider themselves free from the law, until they have completely mastered all these rules for fingering."—H. R. P.

459. *What are some of the principal ways of facilitating the execution of rapid passages?*

First, by changing the fingers whenever a note is repeated, as at (*a*) in the following example; second, by contracting the fingers, as at (*b*); third, by extending the fingers, as at (*c*).

Ex. 225.

460. *What is the proper fingering of the major scales with the right hand?*

In seven scales the thumb falls on Four of the scale, viz.: the scales of C, G, D, A, E, B and F♯ (same as G♭); in two scales—viz.: A♭ and D♭—the thumb falls on Three of the scale; in two scales—viz.: B♭ and E♭—the thumb falls on Two of the scale; in one scale—viz.: the scale of F—the thumb falls on Five of the scale.

461. *What is the proper fingering of the major scales with the left hand?*

In six scales—viz.: the scales of C, G, D, A, E and F—the thumb falls on Five of the scale; in four scales—viz.: B♭, E♭, A♭, D♭ (same as C♯)—the thumb falls on Three of the scale; in two scales—viz.: B and F♯ (same as G♭)—the thumb falls on Four of the scale.

462. *What is the proper fingering of the minor scales?*

The fingering of the minor scales is the same as that of the corresponding major scales, except in the scale of F♯ minor the thumb of the right hand falls on Three of the scale; and in the scales of B♭ minor and E♭ minor, the thumb of the left hand falls on Two of the scale.

NOTE 102.—It will be noticed that, thus far, in our rules for fingering we have made all depend on the *thumb;* there is another scheme (found in Mason & Hoadly's method), in which the distribution of the fingers is made to depend upon the *fourth* finger (next to the last finger). The scales are grouped into three classes, according to the similarity of their fingering, as follows:—

FIRST CLASS: Scales of C, G, D, A and E.

Fingering: { Right Hand, fourth finger on Seven of the scale.
{ Left Hand, fourth finger on Two of the scale.

Ex. 226. C SCALE.   Ex. 227. G SCALE.
Right hand.

Left hand.

Ex. 228. D Scale.   Ex. 229. A Scale.

Right hand.

Left hand.

Ex. 230. E Scale.

Right hand.

Left hand.

NOTE 103.—In these cases it is taken for granted that the thumb follows the fourth finger in outward movement, and that the second and third fingers follow the thumb, and are again followed by the thumb

NOTE 104.—When the right hand ascends, or the left hand descends, it is called *outward* movement; when the right hand descends, or the left hand ascends, it is called *inward* movement. (See Dr. Bidez' "Art of Fingering," pp. 5 and 8.) By using these terms in this sense, we are enabled to give single rules which will apply to both hands.

SECOND CLASS: Scales of B (C♭), F♯ (G♭) and C♯ (D♭).

Fingering : { Right Hand, fourth finger on A♯ or B♭.
{ Left Hand, fourth finger on F♯ or G♭.

(The scales of this class being enharmonic, are here given with both representations.)

Ex. 231. B Scale.   Ex. 232. F♯ Scale.

C♭ Scale.   G♭ Scale.

Ex. 233. C♯ Scale.

D♭ Scale.

THIRD CLASS: Scales of A♭, E♭, B♭ and F.

Fingering: { Right Hand, fourth finger on B♭.
Left Hand, fourth finger on Four of the scale (except the scale
of F, in which it falls on G).

Ex. 234. A♭ SCALE.   Ex. 235. E♭ SCALE.

Ex. 236. B♭ SCALE.   Ex. 237. F SCALE.

NOTE 105.—Mr. W. H. S. suggests that the unusual method of fingering the scales of G, D and A, with the thumb of the left hand on B and E, is easier for the hand, for obvious reasons.

REMARK 10.—*See answer to §448, p. 90, last two clauses.* "I wish something could be said to call attention to the evil results of lifting the fingers too high in Piano-forte practice. Many persons fail to acquire a good touch simply because they fall into this habit. It has its use in moderation and proper proportion, but as a rule, according to many eminent teachers and pianists, the fingers in playing should be held very near the keys; sonority of tone is produced not merely by striking the keys, but by a certain blending or mixture of force, pressure and strength, *combined* with elasticity. This touch is difficult to describe, but the ear can immediately distinguish the effect."—Wm. M.

REMARK 13.—*Page 96, Note 100.* "For illustration of scale passages played with fourth and fifth finger alone, see Chopin's Nocturne, Op. 9, No. 2, in E flat major."—Wm. M.

CHAPTER XIX.

SCALE PLAYING. (Major.)

NOTE 106.—The beauty of scale-playing consists in equality, roundness and uninterrupted continuity; there should not be the slightest indistinctness, nor should there be any appearance of hurrying, or of hesitation; no tone should be more prominent than another, except when it is so intended. Good scale-playing is the *real foundation* for an even, satisfactory and musician-like performance. No one can hope to become a good player who does not devote many hours each week to the diligent and conscientious practice of scales.

As the passing of the thumb under is more difficult than the passing of the fingers over, the ascending scale should be practiced more frequently with the right hand, and the descending with the left hand; each should be practiced separately at first.

NOTE 107.—If the wrist in outward motion be trained to *lead* or glide along in the direction of the scale, thereby bending outward, the elbow remaining steady, the wrist light, it will serve to keep the hand in a more uniform position, facilitate the work and render the scale smoother.

Especial care should be taken in passing the second finger over the thumb to accomplish it without turning the hand out, or lifting the elbow or wrist. The second finger should be curved and raised, passing over the thumb when the thumb strikes, thereby getting into position for its key one note in advance. This can be accomplished with a *light* wrist, steady hand and elbow. In leading the hands outward the second finger, after playing, can lift, curve and be held close to or partly over the third; the third, in its turn, can do similarly with the fourth; thereby helping the preparation for new positions. When practicing the scales inward, the fourth finger can be trained to lift, and move close to or partly over the third finger (after it has played); the third finger can do similarly with regard to the second; thereby again helping the work of preparation for new positions. The thumb should stretch out away from the hand, during inward motion, as soon as released from its key; the fingers and thumb should now do the work of *leading*, the wrist continuing to bend outward. This position of the hand brings the weak fingers squarely over the keys, whether white or black, the thumb near the edge of the white keys. All of these rules are of equal or greater efficiency in the practice of arpeggio-playing.—W. H. S.

NOTE 108.—When both hands are taken together, practice the major scales of C, G, D, A and E first, and in contrary motion, for greater equality in the two hands is to be obtained in this way, because the corresponding fingers and thumbs are passed over and under at the same time. Playing the scales in parallel motion presents some difficulties at first, because this correspondence does not take place (See Remark 14, p. 109). When a wrong key is struck, or false fingering made, the student should begin the scale again, instead of correcting the error where it occurs. In this way only can certainty and accuracy of execution be attained. As soon as the scales can be played in contrary motion and in parallel motion with perfect certainty, the student should practice them in thirds, sixths and tenths. When a firm, even touch has been acquired, the scales should be practiced with different effects of light and shade, particularly with a *crescendo* in ascending and *decrescendo* in descending, thus preparing the way for a rule which is almost universally recognized in musical expression. In crescendo playing carefully guard against the too common habit of hurrying.

NOTE 109.—Especial attention must be given to the thumb in practicing the scales, taking care that it glides along under the fingers as described at Notes 96 and 97, page 95, and this especial attention should be kept up until perfect fluency and facility are attained.

DIATONIC SCALES.

PRELIMINARY STUDIES.

Ex. 238.   Ex. 239.
Ex. 240.   Ex. 241.
Ex. 242.   Ex. 243.
Ex. 244.   Ex. 245.
Ex. 246.   Ex. 247.

MAJOR SCALES.

Ex. 248.   C MAJOR: IN OCTAVES.

NOTE 110.—These Scales may be played through three or four octaves, and with the hands an octave farther apart; they may also be played in contrary motion, i, e., beginning with both hands in the middle of the Key-board and playing in opposite directions and back.

C MAJOR: IN TENTHS.

Ex. 249.

NOTE 111.—To play this Scale in Thirds, take the above example [Tenths] and begin either an octave higher with the left hand, or an octave lower with the right hand.

Ex. 250.   C MAJOR: IN SIXTHS.

Ex. 251.   G MAJOR: IN OCTAVES.

Ex. 252   G MAJOR: IN TENTHS.

NOTE 112.—To play this Scale in Thirds, bring the hands an octave nearer each other in beginning.

Ex. 253.   G Major: in Sixths.

Ex. 254.   D Major: in Octaves.

Ex. 255.   D Major: in Tenths.

Note 113.—To play this Scale in Thirds, bring the hands an octave nearer each other in beginning.

Ex. 256.   D Major: in Sixths.

Ex. 257.   A Major: in Octaves.

A MAJOR: IN TENTHS.

Ex. 258.

NOTE 114.—To play this Scale in Thirds, bring the hands an octave nearer each other in beginning.

Ex. 259.   ### A MAJOR: IN SIXTHS.

Ex. 260.   ### E MAJOR: IN OCTAVES.

Ex. 261.   ### E MAJOR: IN TENTHS.

NOTE 115.—To play this Scale in Thirds, bring the hands an octave nearer each other in beginning.

Ex. 262.   ### E MAJOR: IN SIXTHS.

Ex. 263. B MAJOR: IN OCTAVES.

NOTE 116.—This Scale, being enharmonic with that of C♯ Major, will suffice for both.

Ex. 264. B MAJOR: IN TENTHS.

NOTE 117.—To play this Scale in Thirds, bring the hands an octave nearer each other in beginning.

Ex. 265. B MAJOR: IN SIXTHS.

Ex. 266. G♭ MAJOR: IN OCTAVES.

NOTE 118.—This Scale, being enharmonic with that of F♯ Major, will suffice for both.

Ex. 267. G♭ MAJOR: IN TENTHS.

NOTE 119.—To play this Scale in Thirds, bring the hands an octave nearer each other in beginning.

Ex. 268.   G♭ MAJOR: IN SIXTHS.

Ex. 269.   D♭ MAJOR: IN OCTAVES.

NOTE 120.—This Scale being enharmonic with that of C♯ Major will suffice for both.

Ex. 270.   D♭ MAJOR: IN TENTHS.

NOTE 121.—To play this Scale in Thirds, bring the hands an octave nearer each other in beginning.

Ex. 271.   D♭ MAJOR: IN SIXTHS

Ex. 272.   A♭ MAJOR: IN OCTAVES.

Ab MAJOR: IN TENTHS.

Ex. 273.

NOTE 122.—To play this Scale in Thirds, bring the hands an octave nearer each other in beginning.

Ex. 274.   Ab MAJOR: IN SIXTHS.

Ex. 275.   Eb MAJOR: IN OCTAVES.

Ex. 276.   Eb MAJOR: IN TENTHS.

NOTE 123.—To play this Scale in Thirds, bring the hands an octave nearer each other in beginning

Ex. 277.   Eb MAJOR: IN SIXTHS.

Ex. 278.   B♭ MAJOR: IN OCTAVES.

Ex. 279.   B♭ MAJOR: IN TENTHS.

NOTE 124.—To play this Scale in Thirds, bring the hands an octave nearer each other in beginning.

Ex. 280.   B♭ MAJOR: IN SIXTHS.

Ex. 281.   F MAJOR: IN OCTAVES.

Ex. 282.   F MAJOR: IN TENTHS.

NOTE 125.—To play this Scale in Thirds, bring the hands an octave nearer each other in beginning.

Ex. 283.   F MAJOR: IN SIXTHS.

REMARK 14.—*Page 100, Note 108.* "The scale of D flat major in parallel, as well as contrary motion, is, according to my experience, the easiest to begin with, because of its easy hand-position and uniform motion of the thumb. As being especially applicable to the hand-position belonging to this scale, I refer you to the last sentence but one in Note 107, viz.: 'This position of the hand brings the weak fingers squarely over the keys, whether white or black, the thumb being near the edge of the white keys.' It is maintained by some piano-forte teachers that the chromatic scale is easiest for beginners, on account of the uniformity of fingering."—Wm. M.

Mr. E. S. Hoadly writes:—"An important addition might be made by calling attention to Scales in Canon (first proposed, I think, by Dr. Wm. Mason), in which tenths ascending change to sixths descending, and *vice versa.* (See Mason and Hoadly's System for Beginners, Nos. 140 and 141.)

"Another decided addition would be to impress upon the learner the *great importance of practicing very slowly,* not only at first but in alternation with rapid playing ever afterward. This idea is worth more in the direction of really good progress than any other except flexibility, which also might be enlarged upon to advantage."

CHAPTER XX.

DOUBLE NOTES, (Scales in double Thirds,) etc.

461. *What should be the position of the hands while playing double notes, such as thirds, fourths, sixths, etc?*

The hands should be bent a little outward in the *outward movement,* and a little inward in the *inward movement.* (See Note 104, page 98.)

462. *In playing Thirds, outward, what is the rule for the passing of the fingers?*

When the $\frac{2}{4}$ have been used, the thumb must be passed under the second finger, and the third finger passed over the fourth; when the $\frac{5}{3}$ have been used, the thumb must be passed under the third, and the third over the fifth. In the latter process it is not allowable to raise both, but the connection must be made by expertly turning the third over the fifth.

463. *How are inward Thirds connected?*

In playing Thirds *inward,* after using the $\frac{7}{?}$ the connection with $\frac{2}{4}$ or $\frac{5}{3}$ must be made with the second or third fingers turning over the thumb.

NOTE 126.—In Scales of Sixths, the connection between $\frac{2}{5}$ and $\frac{4}{1}$ is to be made by the second and fourth stretching apart as much as may be, the second gliding off the key in outward motion, the fourth gliding off the key in inward motion; the management of the thumb, however, requires careful study, that smoothness may be attained. The rules for the Scales of Sixths, are equally applicable to Fourths in Chords of the Sixth; and also to Fifths in Chords of the Diminished Seventh. Great care must be taken in playing Thirds, Fourths, and Sixths, that the fingers strike their respective keys at the same instant, so that no separation will be perceptible.

PRELIMINARY EXERCISES.

Ex. 284.   IN THIRDS.

Ex. 285.   In Sixths.

Ex. 286.   C Major: in Thirds.

Ex. 287.   C Major: in Sixths.*

Ex. 288.   G Major: in Thirds.

* The fingering of the Scales in Fourths (R. H.) is nearly the same as that of the Scales in Sixths; e. g.

Ex. 289.

Ex. 290.   G Major: in Sixths.

D Major: in Thirds.

Ex. 291.

D Major: in Sixths.

Ex. 292.

Ex. 293.   A Major: in Thirds.

A Major: in Sixths.

Ex. 294.

Ex. 295. E MAJOR: IN THIRDS.

E MAJOR: IN SIXTHS.

Ex. 296.

Ex. 297. B MAJOR: IN THIRDS.

B MAJOR: IN SIXTHS.

Ex. 298.

Ex. 299. F♯ MAJOR: IN THIRDS.

Ex. 300.　　　F♯ MAJOR: IN SIXTHS.

Ex. 301.　　　D♭ MAJOR: IN THIRDS.

Ex. 302.　　　D♭ MAJOR: IN SIXTHS.

Ex. 303.　　　A♭ MAJOR: IN THIRDS.

Ex. 304.　　　A♭ MAJOR: IN SIXTHS.

E♭ Major: in Thirds.

Ex. 305.

E♭ Major: in Sixths.

Ex. 306.

Ex. 307.   B♭ Major: in Thirds.

B♭ Major: in Sixths.

Ex. 308.

Ex. 309.   F Major: in Thirds.

Ex. 310.   F MAJOR: IN SIXTHS.

NOTE 127.—For the study of Thirds, Fourths, and Sixths, CARL CZERNY'S Toccata, in C Major, Op. 92, will be found invaluable.

REMARK 15.—"For the fingering used in diatonic scales of double thirds and sixths, due credit should be given to Johann Wenzel Tomaschek, 1774–1850, as the author. He was justly esteemed as one of the greatest of piano-forte teachers, and had many very celebrated pupils."—Wm. M.

REMARK 16.—*Special Cases in Thirds.* "I am indebted to Dr. Hans von Bülow for the following interesting fingerings."—A. R. P.

Ascending, only.

Ascending, only.

Descending, only.

Descending, only.

CHAPTER XXI.

SCALE PLAYING, (Minor.)

Ex. 311. A MINOR SCALE.

Ex. 312. E MINOR SCALE.

Ex. 313. B MINOR SCALE.

Ex. 314. F♯ MINOR SCALE.

Ex. 315.   C♯ MINOR SCALE.

Ex. 316.   G♯ MINOR SCALE.

Ex. 317.   E♭ MINOR SCALE.

Ex. 318.   B♭ MINOR SCALE.

Ex. 319.   F MINOR SCALE.

Ex. 320.   C Minor Scale.

Ex. 321.   G Minor Scale.

Ex. 322.   D Minor Scale.

Ex. 323.   A Minor: in Thirds.

Ex. 324.   A Minor: in Sixths.

E MINOR: IN THIRDS.

Ex. 325.

E MINOR: IN SIXTHS.

Ex. 326.

B MINOR: IN THIRDS.

Ex. 327.

B MINOR: IN SIXTHS.

Ex. 328.

F# MINOR: IN THIRDS.

Ex. 329.

F# MINOR: IN SIXTHS.

Ex. 330.

C# MINOR: IN THIRDS.

Ex. 331.

C# MINOR: IN SIXTHS.

Ex. 332.

G# MINOR: IN THIRDS.

Ex. 333.

G# MINOR: IN SIXTHS.

Ex. 334.

Ex. 335.   Eb MINOR: IN THIRDS.

Ex. 336.   Eb MINOR: IN SIXTHS.

Ex. 337.   Bb MINOR: IN THIRDS.

Ex. 338.   Bb MINOR: IN SIXTHS.

Ex. 339.   F MINOR: IN THIRDS.

F MINOR: IN SIXTHS.

Ex. 340.

C MINOR: IN THIRDS.

Ex. 341.

C MINOR: IN SIXTHS.

Ex. 342.

G MINOR: IN THIRDS.

Ex. 343.

G MINOR: IN SIXTHS.

Ex. 344.

Ex. 345.   D MINOR: IN THIRDS.

Ex. 346.   D MINOR: IN SIXTHS.

REMARK. Chapter xxi, page 117. The form of minor scale given in examples 311 to 322 inclusive, is that known as the Melodic Minor Scale. Examples 323 to 346 inclusive are of the form known as the Harmonic Minor Scale. The minor scales in Dr. Mason's Technics are in a mixed form, i. e. Melodic Minor ascending and Harmonic Minor descending. The same is true of the minor Scales in Richardson's Method, from which a whole generation of teachers and their pupils have obtained a wrong idea of the Minor Scales. A simple note at the head of the Chapter on this subject would have obviated the difficulty. The pupil is particularly requested to read the chapter on Minor modes and their Scales beginning on page 36 of this Primer.—H. R. P.

CHAPTER XXII.

SCALE PLAYING, (Chromatic.)

464. *How many modes of fingering the Chromatic Scale are there in general use, and what are they called?*
Three; the French, the English, and the German.

465. *Which is most used?*
The French mode.

466. *For what is the English mode more suitable?*
For light and rapid passages.

467. *Which mode is least used?*
The German or mixed mode.

NOTE 128.—Below we present the three modes of fingering the chromatic scale. That marked (*a*) is the French mode: that marked (*b*) is the English mode, and that marked (*c*) is the German mode. (The French mode, however, is most generally used.)

Ex. 347.

NOTE 129.—The Chromatic Scales in parallel motion should be practiced (through several octaves), both ascending and descending, beginning on each tone of the scale.

The beauty of the Chromatic Scale lies in the gliding succession of tones, perfectly connecting each tone with the next, without jerk or break; the student may also play *crescendo*, ascending, and *decrescendo*, descending. We here insert some chromatic passages, such as occur frequently.

Ex. 348.

Ex. 349.

Ex. 350.

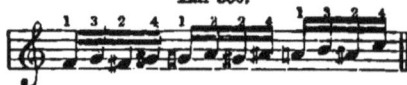

NOTE 130.—Chromatic Sequences of four tones are fingered 1, 2, 3, 4, with the fourth on the outer, and the thumb on the inner, except if the inner tone come on a black key, it must be played with the second finger, thus:—

Ex. 351.

It should be noticed that the inner and outer tones may or may not be the first and last, but whether they are or not, the fingering remains the same, as in the following intricate case of sequence of four tones. (See Dr. Bidez' "Art of Fingering," p. 16.)

Ex. 352.

Ex. 353. CHROMATIC THIRDS (Chord of the Diminished Seventh),

NOTE 131.—The above is the *old* fingering of chromatic thirds. The *new* fingering is better, for the important reason that the same fingering answers for both major and minor chromatic thirds. The new fingering is:—

Ex. 354. MINOR.

Ex. 355. MAJOR.

(The minor thirds are given first as being the easier and more common.)

An analyzation of the scales and their fingering will show their similarity as mentioned above.

In the right hand, in both the minor and major thirds, the *guiding notes* —the notes to be borne in mind—are F♯ and C♯.   Whenever F♯ or C♯ appears as the *lower note* of the third, the fingering is ⅗, the fifth finger being nowhere else introduced.   In the left, in both the minor and major thirds, the *guiding notes* are F and C.   Whenever F or C appears as the *upper note* of the third, whether minor or major, the fingering is ⅗, the fifth finger being nowhere else introduced.   I have found this fingering much the easier in nearly all cases. The very awkward descending chromatic scale in major thirds, which appears in Liszt's "Rigoletto" Fantasie, is greatly simplified and rendered easily possible by this fingering,   Still, as there are cases, chiefly *short* chromatic passages in thirds, in which the old fingering proves very convenient, both fingerings should be studied.—C. F.

NOTE 132. -It is my practice to apply to chromatic thirds, minor and major, the fingering given in Ex. 358 and 359, the convenience and advantages of which appear most manifestly after practicing the following preliminary exercises : —

Preliminary Exercise No. 1.

Ex. 356.

Right hand.

Left hand.

Preliminary Exercise No. 2.

Ex. 357.

Right hand.

Left hand.

Ex. 358. MINOR THIRDS.

Ex. 359. MAJOR THIRDS.

[See remark (a) to Etude, Op. 10, No. 2, of Chopin. Volume I, in Theodore Kullak's edition of Chopin's works.—A. R. P.]

Ex. 361. CHROMATIC FOURTHS. (Chord of the Sixth.)

CHROMATIC FIFTHS AND FOURTHS.
Ex. 362. (Chord of the Diminished Seventh.)

Ex. 363. CHROMATIC SIXTHS.

Ex. 364.   CHROMATIC OCTAVES.

NOTE 134.—See "MASON'S PIANO FORTE TECHNICS," page 107, for instructions in playing *Interlocking Chromatic Octaves*.

CHAPTER XXIII.

ARPEGGIOS AND BROKEN CHORDS.

468. *What is a Chord?*

A union of two or more harmonizing tones, performed simultaneously.

469. *Of what does a Common Chord consist?*

A Common Chord consists of the tone upon which it is founded, called the fundamental tone, together with the tone a third above it, and the tone a fifth above it.

Ex. 365.   COMMON CHORDS.
of C: of G: of D: of A: of E: of B: of F.

470. *How many positions has a Common Chord and what are they called?*

Three; first position, second position and third position.

471. *When is a chord said to be in its first position?*

When its *fundamental* tone is uppermost.

472. *When is a chord said to be in its second position?*

When its *third* is uppermost.

473. *When is a chord said to be in its third position?*

When its fifth is uppermost.

Ex. 366.   DIFFERENT POSITIONS OF THE COMMON CHORD.
Chord of C: Chord of G: Chord of A.

1st pos. 2nd. 3rd. 1st pos. 2nd. 3rd. 1st pos. 2nd. 3rd.

474. *What are Arpeggios?*

The tones of a chord performed in regular succession instead of being performed simultaneously.

Ex. 367.   CHORDS BROKEN INTO ARPEGGIOS.
Chords of C: Arpeggios.   Chords of G:

1st pos.   2nd pos.   1st pos.   2nd pos.   3rd pos.   1st pos.

Arpeggios.　　　Chords of A:　　　Arpeggios.

3rd pos.　　1st pos.　　2nd pos.　3rd pos,　2nd pos.　　3rd pos.

475. *What are Broken Chords?*

The tones of a chord performed in irregular succession.

Ex. 368.　　　　　BROKEN CHORDS.

NOTE 134.—The student will have no trouble in discerning the difference between Arpeggios and Broken Chords if it be kept in mind that Arpeggios are a *regular* succession, and Broken Chords are an *irregular* succession of tones, however, they are frequently used as synonymous terms.

NOTE 135.—In playing Arpeggios and Broken Chords, the hand must be more extended than in scale-playing; the student should study carefully the fingering as here laid down. There are three chords which serve as models with respect to the fingerings of Arpeggios and Broken Chords, as follows:

I.—Chord of C major: Model for all that have three white keys or three black keys:

Ex. 369.　　　　　FIRST MODEL.
Primary Chords.　　　*Arpeggios.*

1st Position.　　2nd Position.

3rd Position.

NOTE 136.—In order to save space only one staff is used. The fingering *above* is for the Right Hand; that *below* for the Left Hand. The Groups must be smoothly connected, as indicated.

Ex. 370.　　　　　FIRST GROUPING.

R.H.
L.H.

Ex. 371.　　　　　SECOND GROUPING.

R.H.
L.H.

Ex. 372　　　　　THIRD GROUPING. (a).

R.H.
L.H.

Ex. 373.   THIRD GROUPING.   (b).

NOTE 137.—The fingering given in the Third Grouping (a) and (b) applies to the Major and Minor chords of all other keys.

Ex. 374.   FOURTH GROUPING.

NOTE 138.—Practice the above exercise in keys of G, F, and F♯ Major; A, E, D, and E♭ Minor, with the same fingering.

II.—Chords of D Major; Model for all that have one black key (except B♭ Major, and B Minor.)

Ex. 375.   SECOND MODEL.
Primary Chords.   *Arpeggios.*

1st Position.   2nd Position. 3rd Position.

Ex. 376.   FIRST GROUPING.

NOTE 139.—In chords of D, 1st position, left hand, some will find it easier to use the 3rd finger on the black key.   This is only allowable in D, A, and E Major.   The same is true for right hand in C, G & F (minor), 3d pos.

Ex. 377.   SECOND GROUPING.

NOTE 140.—For Third Grouping, see Third Grouping of the chords of C, above.

Ex. 378.   FOURTH GROUPING.

NOTE 141.—Practice the above exercises in the keys of A and E Major; G, C, and F Minor, with the same fingering.

III.—Chord of E♭ Major: Model for all that have two black keys (except B Major, and B♭ Minor.)

Ex. 379.   THIRD MODEL.

1st Position.   2nd Position. 3rd Position.

Ex. 380.   FIRST GROUPING.

NOTE 142.—Here also in first position, left hand, many use the 3rd finger instead of the 4th; in Minor chords only the 4th must be used.

NOTE 143.—For Second and Third Grouping see those of the chord of C.

Ex. 381.   FOURTH GROUPING.

NOTE 144.—The following are the four exceptions mentioned above, viz: B♭ Major, B Minor, B Major, and B♭ Minor.

Ex. 382.   B♭ MAJOR. *8va..........*

Ex. 383.   B MINOR. *8va..........*

Ex. 384.   B MAJOR. *8va..........*

Ex. 385.   B♭ MINOR. *8va..........*

476. *What are Grand Arpeggios?*
Grand Arpeggios are those which sweep through several octaves.

477. *What general rules must be kept in mind while playing Grand Arpeggios?*
The hand must be more extended than in scale-playing; the thumb must glide along under the fingers, as in scale-playing; the arm must be held a little from the body; all motion of the elbow and twisting of the arm must be avoided; and no finger must be allowed to remain on its key. (See Note 110, page 102, which will apply with as much force, and in greater degree, to arpeggio as to scale-playing!)

NOTE 145.—The smooth connection of tones becomes more difficult than in Scale-playing because of the greater stretch of the hand, therefore the player must pay particular and continual attention to such connections.

NOTE 146.—If in such cases the distance between notes be too great or the fingers too short, they can be trained, in leaving a key, to glide off from it mildly, straightening out first to increase the facility of spanning the interval! But the finger next playing should *not* glide to its key! Care should *always* be taken to approach the keys from a point perpendicular to that portion of the key which is to be struck.—W. H. S.

NOTE 147.—The following exercises must be practiced in exact time, so that the rhythmical accents will fall on different fingers. The chords of C, D, and E♭ Major again serve as models of fingering.

GRAND ARPEGGIOS.

Ex. 389.   D MAJOR: 1st POSITION.

D MAJOR: 2nd POSITION

Ex. 390.

D MAJOR: 3rd POSITION.

Ex. 391.

NOTE 148.—In E♭ Major, as in all other chords having 2 black keys, the thumb always comes upon the single white one. Each position therefore is referred back to the second. But it is well also to practice some of these chords, (B♭ Major 1st position, E♭ Major 3rd position, B Major 3rd position, etc.,) with the fingering of C Major, (that is, with the thumb upon the black keys.)

NOTE 149.—For further study and practice in Arpeggios, the student is referred to Dr. Mason's "Piano-Forte Technics," page 73. Here are nearly thirty large pages devoted to the study of Arpeggios, beginning (where we have just left off) with chords of the diminished seventh and their various harmonic changes, which are set forth in a series of exercises in every variety of rhythmic forms, accenting in fours, sixes, eights, nines, twelves, sixteens, eighteens, etc., arranged for right hand, for left hand, for right and left alternately, for both hands in parallel motion, in contrary motion, in canon form, etc., etc. Also the many *accent* exercises.

The following studies are also recommended for acquiring facility in all possible kinds of *arpeggio* playing:—
Clementi's "Gradus ad Parnassum," Nos. 12, 24, 30.
Cramer's "Exercises" (Peters' Edition), Nos. 5, 12, 15, 18, 21, 23, 24, 27, 33, 38, 46, 56.
Czerny's "L'Art de délier les Doigts," Op. 740, Nos. 2, 6, 12, 14, 15, 26, 31, 36, 46, 47, 50.
For extended *Arpeggios*, see Chopin's "Studies," Op. 10, Nos. 1 and 11; Op. 25, Nos. 1 and 12; and the "Studies" of Ferdinand Hiller, Ignaz Moscheles, Stephen Heller, Sigismund Thalberg, Ludwig Berger, Franz Liszt, &c. All these "Studies," however, are for more advanced performers; for beginners, the "Twelve Arpeggio Studies" by A. Krause are very recommendable.

CHAPTER XXIV.

OCTAVE PLAYING.

"Within the last forty or fifty years the fashion of octave playing has changed very much for the better. Before that time octaves were played by movements of the fore-arm, the wrist remaining rigid. This mode of octave playing is open to several objections, the most important of which are that owing to the rigid condition of the wrist, it is very fatiguing ; and that, for the same reason, it produces a bad tone. The present mode of playing octaves is from the hand, the wrist remaining perfectly flexible at the moment of attack. In this way the piano-forte is made to give out its full tone without unduly fatiguing the player. This mode has also the advantage of appearing more graceful and easy.

The prime conditions of good octave playing are two; (1.) perfect flexibility of the wrist, and (2.) a firm touch with the thumb and little finger.

When the hand is expanded to the compass of an octave, certain muscles are called into action which have a tendency to hold the wrist in a rigid state, by their sympathetic action on muscles not properly employed in this exercise.

The first point in octave playing is to become familiar with the sensation of a flexible wrist. The first keys are to be struck *firmly*, with a blow of the hand, moving from the wrist, the thumb and fifth finger *clinging to the key*, while the wrist is to be completely relaxed. Every note of the following exercise is to be played in this way, allowing ample time for fully completing the various motions required and experiencing the corresponding sensations:

Ex. 392.

Before playing the following exercise, the hand is to be swung loosely from the wrist, like a flail, fifteen or twenty times, leaving the wrist absolutely as loose as if the hinge were made of string or leather, instead of bone and cartilage. The first key is to be struck with a blow of the hand, and the following four are to be played as if the hand were rebounding from the blow in a manner analogous to the repeated rebounding of a rubber ball, after being forcibly thrown against the floor. Play with the right hand alone, allowing long intervals of rest."

Ex. 393.

For a continuation of this System of Octave playing see "MASON'S PIANO-FORTE TECHNICS," page 104.

NOTE 150.—In this connection it would be well for the player to practice accurate wrist movements with one finger playing at a time, using every finger in turn. The motion to be that of octave playing, the finger to be trained to a steady, unchanging form of its own, in fact kept rigid! This can be seldom be successfully acquired without making slow motions of the hand, during which the player's energy must be concentrated on keeping the finger from independent movements of its own! This practice is a means of gaining independence of the fingers and wrist, and will make one's touch more firm or crisp for octave and staccato playing.—W. H. S.

Prof. PLAIDY says : "The study of this method of touch by means of the loose wrist is indispensable to the technicalities of piano-forte playing, in order to acquire a light execution, and a beautiful and free effect of sound. In order to obviate the clumsy, heavy touch, common to beginners, and acquire lightness and ease, the following exercises should be played *softly* and *slowly*. At first they will be fatiguing, therefore, the student must not practice them long, but frequently, until strength and steadiness is acquired."

Ex. 394.

Ex. 395.

NOTE 151.—When Octaves are to be played slowly, the following fingering may be employed :

Ex. 396.

Scale of C Major.

Ex. 397.
Or this :

NOTE 152.—When octaves are to be played rapidly, they must be connected as well as possible by a skillful gliding of the thumb and fingers, using the 3rd and 4th fingers on the black keys, also by passing the 3rd and 4th fingers over the 5th in outward movement, and the 5th under the 4th and 3rd in inward movement.

Ex. 398.

Scale of Db Major.

Ex. 399.

Scale of B Major.

Ex. 400.

NOTE 153.—The following four formulas should be transposed into other keys.

Ex. 401.

I.   II.   III.   IV.

NOTE 154.—The following fourteen formulas should also be transposed into other keys.

Ex. 402.

V.   VI.   VII.   VIII.

IX.   X.   XI.

XII.   XIII.   XIV.

XV.   XVI.   XVII.   XVIII.

Ex. 406.

Ex. 407.

NOTE 155.—There is no general rule which applies to the use of the 4th finger on the black keys in staccato octave passages. If the hand be wide, the 4th finger will generally be used. If the hand be small, the 4th finger will only be used when it is most convenient. In all cases the intelligent teacher will give directions suitable to the individual peculiarities of each pupil.

Ex. 408.

Ex. 409.

Ex. 410.

Ex. 411.

Ex. 412.

Ex. 413.

The following three formulas should be practiced descending also.

Ex. 414.

NOTE 156.—For Playing Broken Octaves. Arch the hand, covering the keys of an octave, from the thumb to the fifth finger, as indicated in the note on octave-playing. Keep the thumb, and the side of the wrist next the thumb *down*, lifting the rest of the hand, keeping the fifth finger rigid in its curved and erect form, play many times with the fifth finger in this way holding the thumb on the key, and making as full a motion up and down with the rest of the hand as possible. Then hold the fifth finger down in turn, with the outside of the wrist low, and roll the thumb side of the hand up and down, playing with the thumb: afterward alternate with the extremes in broken octave practice. This method gives stronger and bolder results than that in ordinary use, and may be termed a *wrist-exercise*. It helps loosen the wrist, and at the same time gives the weak fingers a great power of motion. The fourth finger should then be substituted for the fifth, observing the same rules as before indicated.—W. H. S.

NOTE 157.—Additional studies for perfecting "wrist playing" will be found in the works of Dreyschock, Kullak, Ch. Mayer, and others. The following are also recommended:—

Clementi's "Gradus ad Parnassum," No. 65 (Tausig's Edition, No. 26).
Czerny's No. 33 of Op. 740.
Moscheles' "Study in E flat minor," Op. 70.
Hummel's Op. 125, No. 8.
Hummel's Op. 18 (the latter part of the Fantasia).
Kessler's No. 8.
Hiller's Nos. 1, 5, 24.
Chopin's Op. 25, No. 10.
Beethoven's Op. 54 (First Movement).

CHAPTER XXV.

PEDALS.

478. *For what is the Soft Pedal used?*

For the purpose of diminishing the volume of sound. (*For description of the Soft Pedal see Note* 78, *page* 87.)

479. *How is the use of the Soft Pedal indicated?*

By the words *Una Corda*.

NOTE 160.—The Grand Piano formerly had but two strings to each key, and by a mechanical contrivance, the Soft Pedal shifted the key-board and action to the right, so that each hammer would strike but one string (*una corda*.) Modern Grand Pianos have three strings to each key, so that shifting the action by means of the soft pedal leaves two strings of the unison to vibrate instead of three, still the term, *una corda*, is retained.

480. *How is the discontinuance of the Soft Pedal indicated?*

By the words *tre corde* (three strings) or the abbreviation T. C.

NOTE 161.—The use of the Soft Pedal is frequently left to the taste of the performer; it *must* be used when indicated by the mark *una corda*, and *may* be used in all passages requiring a delicate effect. Beginners must follow the directions given by their teacher with regard to the use of the Pedals.

481. *For what is the Damper Pedal used?*

NOTE 162.—This Pedal is frequently miscalled the Loud Pedal.

For the purpose of prolonging the sound after the fingers have been removed from the keys.

482. *What is the primary use of the Damper Pedal?*

To prolong the base tone while the chord belonging to it is played.

483. *How is the use of the Damper Pedal indicated?*

By the mark "Ped."

484. *How is the discontinuance of the Damper Pedal indicated?*

By the asterisk ✳.

NOTE 163.—Some composers—notably F. HILLER, in a "Bolero" which I have of his—have introduced an additional, and very useful mark in connection with the Damper-Pedal. In long passages, where the pedal is to be used throughout, and changed with each chord, they write "Ped" at the beginning, and put the mark ◊ wherever the pedal is to be instantaneously released and used again. There is frequently not room enough for "✳, Ped" at every such place, especially when they are of rapid occurrence, and this mark fills a needed gap in musical short-hand. When the Pedal is finally released the usual mark "✳" is used.—C. F.

NOTE 164.—The student should *never touch the Damper Pedal until instructed by a careful teacher*. An indiscriminate use of this Pedal produces an effect which is vile beyond all description, and which cannot be too severely condemned. (The pupil should read and inwardly digest Note 78, page 87.)

485. *May the Damper Pedal and the Soft Pedal be used together ?*

They may ; instead of being antagonistic as is commonly supposed, they frequently require to be used at the same time.

NOTE 165.—The supposition that the Damper Pedal and the Soft Pedal are antagonistic, undoubtedly arises from the name "*Loud Pedal*," commonly given to the Damper Pedal, and as *Loud* is opposed to *Soft*, the idea readily obtains that the two pedals are similarly opposed.

NOTE 166.—"I believe that we are indebted to MR. WM. H. SHERWOOD for suggesting and teaching the simplest and clearest method of marking pedal effects that has yet come into use. This plan consists simply in writing a perfectly straight line ascending obliquely from the spot on the paper corresponding to the time at which the pedal should be pressed and ending where the pedal should drop. Such a mark may be written in or below the bass, or if the pedal has more especial reference to notes in the upper parts, attention can be called to that fact by writing the line near those notes. We may express by it that the pedal is to be taken just before, exactly with, or at any space after a given note. We may show that the pedal is to drop and instantly and suddenly rise again by making a little jog in the line, and if it ever should be required to write the pedal for a very long passage where the line could not conveniently extend, a very rare and improbable situation, we have still the expression 'Sempre pedale' open to use. Nothing could be simpler or more perfect, and it is certainly to be hoped that composers and publishers will speedily adopt this notation and adhere to it exclusively."—HENRY G. HANCHETT. *From an essay in the Art Journal on "The Proper use of Pedals."*

NOTE 167.—The ordinary artistic use of the Damper Pedal may be represented as follows :—

EX. 415.   FIRST PHRASE OF " OLD HUNDRED."

This example is represented in $\frac{6}{4}$ measure, for the purpose of analyzing the alternate use of the fingers and pedal. The result is the *legato* blending of tone from one chord to another without blurring.

Again:—

EX. 416.   FROM THE FIRST OF MENDELSSOHN'S SONGS WITHOUT WORDS.

There are two modifications frequently practical, viz:—

1st. In case of Arpeggio chords, as follows:—(*From Schumann's Nocturne in F.*)

Ex. 417.

Schumann writes (*con pedale.*)

etc.

Ped.

In this case it is desirable to make the lowest and highest tones of each chord strongest. (In all such cases, I should try to make the fundamental base tones stronger than intermediate parts—a good rule for ordinary harmony any way.)

2nd. Modification :

Ex. 418.

etc.

Allegretto.

pp

etc.

Ped.

(The above is from Chopin's Prelude in A flat, Opus 21, No. 17.)

In the case of extended arpeggio chords, we need the pedal down at the outset before losing the tone of the first notes played. This necessitates raising the pedal *before the time of such chords.* (See the oblique lines in Example 417.)

In the second example, the strongly accented bass note can be made to continue sounding through several abrupt changes of the pedal, which will, however, quickly clear up the blurring of the softly played upper tones and chords. (See Example 418.)—W. H. S.

NOTE 168.—For the study of the pedals, the student will find Liszt's transcriptions of Schubert's Songs; Chopin's Nocturnes; Moscheles' Studies, Op. 70; Mendelssohn's Songs Without Words; Thalberg's Fantasias, and Art of Singing; and Beethoven's Sonata, Op. 27, (Moonlight Sonata,) of great assistance.

CHAPTER XXVI.

A CHAPTER OF ADVICE AND CAUTION.

The question is frequently asked of the author: "How young should a child begin to study instrumental music?"

As soon as a child can count to eight, can distinguish the right hand from the left, knows black from white, knows the letters of the alphabet as far as G, can understand the relation of a whole to a half or a half to a whole, that child is old enough to commence (in a small way) the study of the piano or organ. The most illustrious players are generally those who began very young.

However, it should be kept in mind that young children should not be fatigued by long lessons or long practice; a few minutes each day, during the first year, will be quite sufficient; gradually increasing the length of both lessons and daily practice during the first three or four years. Some children will comprehend a lesson clearly and quickly, and will, consequently, progress rapidly; such should not be held back; but others, on the contrary, may require many lessons on a single principle; such should not be discouraged by expressions of contempt or impatience, for it should be remembered that in all branches of art and literature, many who at the beginning have appeared dull and even stupid, have nevertheless subsequently distinguished themselves.

The importance of a *correct* beginning cannot be too strongly urged; hence, in the purchase of an instrument, *superiority of tone* and *excellence of action* should be considered of first importance, and the price to be paid as secondary. "The better the instrument, the more it will aid the pupil's progress. If means be scanty, as is often the case, better endeavor to save in some other way, than use a bad instrument for the sake of economy." It is scarcely necessary to say that the pupil's musical feeling and zeal for study, are greatly increased by an instrument of fine tone and action. In selecting an instrument, do not be deceived by filigree mouldings and a beautiful polish, for such things, however they may enhance the value of the instrument as a *piece of furniture,* do not add one whit to its *real excellence,* which consists of pure *quality* as regards *tone,* and superior workmanship as regards *action.* I once witnessed the sale of a piano, which would have been very sad, had it not been so superlatively ridiculous. A man and his wife wished an instrument for their daughter; they were shown one which was made by one of the best makers. It had an exquisite tone and delightful action, but was plain; the case was not even veneered, but was grained in close imitation of rosewood. The manufacturers, however, had spared no expense upon its "true inwardness." By its side stood an instrument which was evidently little better than so much kindling-wood; as far as tone was concerned it could hardly be called a piano, but it had a deep polish, elaborately carved legs, plinth-mouldings, inlaid name-board, and that abomination—*pearl keys*. The dealer offered this bauble for $100 less than the other, and although the daughter, who was something of a player, urged them to take the plain instrument, they positively purchased the trinket, and, I presume, congratulated them-selves upon getting a *beautiful* instrument.

The importance which our great musicians attach to proper instruc-tion at the beginning is shown by the following extracts :

"We must play with the fingers bent, and the sinews free from all stiffness. He who plays with the fingers stretched out, and the sinews stiff, experiences, besides the naturally consequent awkwardness, a particular evil, inasmuch as he removes the fingers too far from the thumb (which should always be as near them as possible) and takes from it all possibility of doing its duty."—EMANUEL BACH.

"Let the fingers and thumb be placed over the keys, always ready to strike, bending them more or less, in proportion to their length, and accommodating them to the exigencies of the black and white keys."—CLEMENTI.

"The second, third, and fourth fingers must be bent so as to bring the thumb and the fifth finger on a line; each finger must be placed over its respective key and remain in that position, whether used or not."—J. B. CRAMER.

"Excepting in extensions, the fingers must neither stand too far apart, nor be drawn too closely together; each finger should lie naturally over its proper key."—HUMMEL.

"Keep the keys down the full length of every note, for when the contrary is required, it is indicated by a particular sign. All unnec-essary motion must be avoided."—CLEMENTI.

"The extremities of the fingers (but not the nails) must strike the keys; their motion should be so smooth as not to be noticed."—CRAMER.

"The quickness of motion lies only in the joints of the fingers, which should move with lightness and freedom. The fingers should not change their naturally bent position. The *touch* or mode of striking a key must be decisive and equal. All pushing and thumping are to be avoided. The fingers must not rest longer on the keys than the prescribed time."—HUMMEL.

"Each finger must be lifted exactly at the same instant in which the next finger strikes its key. In scale passages, the fingers, when not playing, must be held exactly over the middle of one of the five con-tiguous keys. When one finger strikes, the others must not move, and each finger, after being used, must return to its previous situation."—CZERNY.

" We should especially accustom children, when necessary, to stretch the hand as much as possible, instead of jumping backward and forward with the whole hand, in doing which, moreover, the fingers are often drawn together as in a lump."—EMANUEL BACH.

"Apropos of Stein's little girl, whoever can see and hear her play, without laughing, must be like her father—stein (stone). When she has a passage to execute she lifts her arm into the air, and if it requires any particular emphasis, it is done with the arm, and not with the finger, and in the heaviest and worst possible manner. When a passage occurs which ought to flow as smoothly as oil, and, of course, requires that the fingers should be changed, she gives herself no concern on that point, but lifts her hand and begins again quite at her ease. She might become clever; she possesses talent, but on this plan she will never acquire rapidity, because she pursues the very best method to make the hand heavy. The most necessary, difficult, though the principal thing in music, namely, the *time*, she will never acquire, if she is accustomed from infancy to play out of time. I have talked with her father on this subject and have made a convert of him."—W. A. MOZART.

" On commencing a new piece, and particularly a *study*, the player is recommended:

1st. To play the piece slowly, and with great care, and pay strictest attention, not to omit a single note or accidental.

2d. Whenever the fingering is marked, not to deviate from it.*

3d. To give each note in the division of a measure its proper value, and make one hand correspond *strictly* with the other.

4th. To practice separately, again and again, and always with a distinct touch, such passages, measures, and even single notes, as present any difficulties of execution.

5th. To play the piece over several times for the express purpose of fully understanding and executing all the marks which relate to character, expression and style."—MOSCHELES.

" Some persons play stickily, as if they had glue between their fingers. Their touch may be called too long, for they let the notes last beyond their time. Others play too shortly, as if the keys were red-hot. That is also bad; the medium is better. All sorts of touch are good when in the right place."—EMANUEL BACH.

" The style of a performance should be a true image of that of the composition. It is necessary, therefore, to study the character of a piece before we attempt to execute it."—CLEMENTI.

" Unbecoming habits should be carefully avoided, as holding the face too close to the book, biting the lips, nodding the head to mark the time, opening or distorting the mouth, etc., etc., as they are prejudicial to health and contrary to gracefulness of demeanor."—HUMMEL.

---

* A teacher may sometimes discover a different mode of fingering, which will produce an equally good effect, and at the same time be more peculiarly adapted to the hand of the pupil.

"The player must possess such control over his fingers as enables him by the weight and pressure of their extremities to produce every shade and gradation of tone from the most delicate to the most powerful."—Moscheles.

"We must not rest until we have succeeded in acquiring *fire* without violence, *power* without harshness, *sweetness* without languor. The pianist must endeavor to make his hands so independent of each other that he may be able to play the loudest and most impassioned passages with one, while the other plays with the greatest softness and tranquility. Sometimes it is even necessary to employ two contrary expressions with the same hand. Learn to diversify your expression, let the melody predominate, and do not allow the accompanying parts to stifle it."—Kalkbrenner.

"To obtain great execution, combined with fulness and variety of tone, all stiffness must be avoided; suppleness of the wrist, and elasticity in the pliancy of the fingers, are indispensable. Avoid the affectation and bad taste of constantly retarding the tones of the melody after those of the accompaniment, thus producing the effect of a continuous syncopation which the composer never intended. In a slow melody, with notes of long duration, it is expedient, at the commencement of a phrase, to attack the singing part after the base, but with a difference almost imperceptible.

"One of the most important recommendations we can urge, is that each tone be held (the keys kept down) its full value, unless the contrary be indicated. For this purpose, fingering of substitution must be employed, especially in music of several parts.

"To avoid hurrying, and playing over fast, is much more difficult than is generally imagined.

"Let us advise all young performers to refrain from all unnecessary motion of the body, and preserve an easy deportment of the arms; not to place themselves in too high a position in respect to the key-board; let them listen well to their own performance, question themselves, be severe in judging of themselves. In general they work too much with their fingers and not with sufficient intelligence."—S. Thalberg.

"Many players, in scale practice, allow the first finger of the right hand ascending, and the first finger of the left hand descending, to linger on its key; great care must be taken to avoid this fault. Carefully avoid exaggeration of feeling and expression; too strong accentuation; want of rhythmical feeling; indistinctness in execution; changing the time; hurrying, dragging, slurring, thumping, want of evenness in the movement of the hands; swinging the body about; flinging the hands into the air; interpolation of strange passages; failing to heed the composers' marks of expression; unnecessary doubling of the notes when they are written single; and, not least of all, playing *arpeggiando* when the chords are to be struck simultaneously.

"Two faults which cannot be too carefully guarded against, are: (1) Practicing a rapid movement in too quick a tempo; and (2) Playing the easy passages of a work as frequently as the difficult ones; this is not only a waste of time, but prejudicial to true musical development; yet many players find it difficult to rid themselves of these bad habits.

"A man's merit consists only in the amount of industry and exertion he bestows upon the object he desires to attain. He that is gifted by nature with talent or genius, has no right to look upon these gifts as his own desert, but as an obligation, which Heaven has imposed upon him, to cultivate them so far as to enable him to perform all that may be reasonably expected from the talent he possesses."—Louis Plaidy.

Many players who are deficient in precision, correctness, and clearness, attempt to conceal their want of skill by means of the Damper Pedal. This vile practice cannot be too severely condemned. The pupil should never use this pedal until it has been carefully studied under the guidance of an intelligent teacher.

CHAPTER XXVII.

TECHNICAL EXERCISES, STUDIES, SONATAS, Etc.

For technical exercises, which are thoroughly systematic in design, and exhaustive in treatment, we would heartily recommend Dr. Mason's "Piano-Forte Technics." If others are wanted, Plaidy's "Technical Studies," and Czerny's "Forty Daily Exercises," will be found useful.

The following list of "Studies," together with the graded series of "Sonatas," is by ERNEST PAUER.

Among the studies for beginners, we recommend :—

Brunner, C. T., Op. 412.
Chwatal, F. X., Op. 105.
Czerny, Carl, Op. 139.
Schmitt, Aloys., Op. 16.
Clementi, Muzio, " Preludes and Exercises."
Köhler, L., Op. 151 ; Op. 50 ; Op. 152.
Berens, H., Op. 61 ; Op. 73 ; Op. 79 (for children).
Gurlitt, C., Op. 50, 51, 52, and 53.
Krug, D., Op. 213.
Enckhausen, Op. 63.
Czerny, C., Op. 353.
Duvernoy, J. B., Op. 176.
Lemoine, Op. 37.
Czerny, C., Op. 299, "School of Velocity."
Bertini, H., Op. 100.
Heller, S., Op. 47,
Löschhorn, A., Op. 66.

For more advanced performers :—

Heller, S., Op. 45 ; Op. 46.
Krause, A., Op. 2.
Bertini, H., Op. 29 ; Op. 32.
Czerny, C., Op. 740.
Grund, C., Op. 21.
Clementi, Toccata in B flat.
Pollini, F., Toccata in G major.
Onslow, G., Toccata in C major.
Czerny, C., Op. 92, Toccata in C major.

Mayer, Carl, Toccata in E major.
Moscheles, I., Op. 73.
Bach, J. S., Fifteen Inventiones; Fifteen Symphonies.
Müller, A. E., Caprices (1—15).
Cramer, J. B., "Studio."
Clementi, M., "Gradus ad Parnassum."
Mayer, Carl, Op. 200; Op. 119.
Kessler, J., Op. 20.
Döring, Op. 24; Op. 30, "Rhythmical Studies."
Köhler, L., Op. 128, "New School of Velocity."
Löschhorn, A., Op. 67.

For very advanced performers:—

Köhler, L., Op. 112.
Czerny, C., "The School of the Legato and Staccato."
Heller, S., Op. 16.
Seeling, H., Op. 10.
Hiller, F., Op. 15.
Taubert, W., Op. 40.
Goldschmidt, O., Op. 13.
Bennett, W. S., Op. 11.
Berger, L., Op. 12; Op. 22.
Moscheles, I., Op. 70.
Kalkbrenner, F., Op. 145.
Chopin, F., Op. 10; Op. 25.
Moscheles, I., Op. 95.
Henselt, A., Op. 2; Op. 5.
Schumann, R., Op. 13; Toccata, Op. 7.
Döhler, T., "Twelve Studies."
Thalberg, S., Op. 26; "Three Studies."
Schumann, R., "Paganini's Caprices," Op. 3; Op. 10.
Mendelssohn, F., Op. 35, "Preludes and Fugues;" "Three
    Studies;" "Three Preludes."
Bach, J. S., "Forty-eight Preludes and Fugues."
Liszt, F., "Three Studies;" "Six Caprices de Paganini; "Études
    d'une éxecution transcendante."
"New Gradus ad Parnassum; One Hundred Studies by different
    Composers."

For those who are beginning the study of *sonatas*, the excellent easy
sonatas by A. Krause, Taubert, and C. Reinecke, offer valuable material,
after which the following may be taken up in the order in which they
are here given :—

Emanuel Bach (Edition of Leuckart in Leipzig, or in Farrenc's
    "Trésor du Pianiste.")
Sonatinas by Clementi.
Sonatinas by Kuhlau.
Sonatas by Haydn.
Sonatas by Mozart.　As the number of Mozart's Sonatas differ
    in the various editions, the thematic beginning is here
    given :—

No. 16, in C.

No. 1, in C.

No. 17, in F.

No. 2, in F.

No. 18, in B♭.

No. 10, in C.

No. 5, in G.

No. 3, in B♭.

No. 6, in D.

No. 12, in F.

No. 13, in B♭.

No. 4, in E♭.

Sonatas by Clementi.
Sonatas by Dussek.
Caprices by A. E. Müller.
Sonatas by J. N. Hummel.
Sonatas by Beethoven, Nos. 19, 20, 25, 9, 10, 1, 2, 3, 6, 5, 7, 8, 4, 11, 15, 12, 13, 14, 16, 17, 18.
Sonatas by C. M. von Weber, Nos. 1, 4, 3, 2.
Sonatas by Franz Schubert, Nos. 3, 4, 2, 5, 7, 1, 8, 6, 10, 9.
Sonatas by Beethoven, Nos. 22, 21, 24, 23, 27, 26, 28, 30, 31, 32, 29.

CHAPTER XXVIII.

PLAN FOR PIANO FORTE CLASSES.

"A class should consist of three pupils, who are to study the same piece and to share an hour's lesson at one Piano-forte. The three pupils should be as nearly equal in musical capability as possible. Each pupil is to be twenty minutes at the piano, during which time the other two are to observe carefully all that is done and said, and when necessary, to ask any further explanation they may think needful.

In order to thoroughly equalize the progress of each pupil, care must be taken that whatever new music is read, or whatever pieces are played by a particular pupil at one lesson, shall be read and played by the others at succeeding lessons. When the new lesson is first read, the teacher is to mark the fingering, and anything else that may be necessary on the music of the pupil then at the piano; after the hour's lesson, and before separating, the other two pupils are to transcribe all such fingering, etc., on their own copies. Among the advantages of this plan are:—

1. The expense is only one-third that of private lessons.

2. The pupils obtain all necessary fingering and explanations as effectually as by private lessons.

3. The fact of each pupil having to play in the presence of the two others must necessarily assist in the acquirement of that self-possession indispensable to an intelligible performance of a piece.

4. All the advantage to be gained by hearing the teacher play the pieces that are studied can be at once equally obtained by the three pupils."—AGUILAR.

" The learners of the second chapter should be the teachers of the first, while the master should occasionally inspect their examples—it is also recommended that an examination of the whole school should take place at stated periods. Pupils of talent should be removed to the higher classes as soon as the master finds them qualified, without waiting for those who are less rapid in their improvement. The exercise of each should be appointed by the master. They may be selected either from the Primer, or by making the pupils explain the lesson about to be played, pointing out the notes from which the fingers should be raised, and those which are to be held down; manner of counting, the reasons for the fingering, etc. The younger pupils should be attended at their daily practice by one of the older ones, who is to be appointed by the master."—BURROWS.

CHAPTER XXIX.

SIXTY-EIGHT RULES FOR YOUNG BEGINNERS.

By ROBERT SCHUMANN.

1. The most important thing is to cultivate the sense of Hearing. Take pains early to distinguish Tones and Keys by the Ear. The bell, the window-pane, the cuckoo,—seek to find what tones they each give out.

2. You must sedulously practise Scales and other finger exercises. But there are many persons who imagine all will be accomplished if they keep on spending many hours each day, till they grow old, in mere mechanical practice. It is about as if one should busy himself daily with repeating the A-B-C as fast as possible, and always faster and faster. Use your time better.

3. "Dumb piano-fortes," so called, or key-boards without sound, have been invented. Try them long enough to see that they are good for nothing. You cannot learn to speak from the dumb.

4. Play in time! The playing of many virtuosos is like the gait of a drunkard. Make not such your models.

5. Learn betimes the fundamental laws of Harmony.

6. Be not frightened by the words, *Theory, Thorough Bass, Counter-point,* etc.; they will meet you friendlily if you meet them so.

7. Never dilly-dally over a piece of music, but attack it briskly, and never play it only half through!

8. Dragging and hurrying are equally great faults.

9. Strive to play easy pieces well and beautifully; it is better than to render harder pieces only indifferently well.

10. Always insist on having your instrument purely tuned.

11. You must not only be able to play your little pieces with the fingers; you must be able to hum them over without a piano. Sharpen your imagination so that you may fix in your mind not only the Melody of a composition, but also the Harmony belonging to it.

12. Accustom yourself, even though you have but little voice, to sing at sight without the aid of an instrument. The sharpness of your hearing will continually improve by that means. But if you are the possessor of a rich voice, lose not a moment's time, but cultivate it, and consider it the fairest gift which heaven has lent you.

13. You must carry it so far that you can understand a piece of music upon paper.

14. When you are playing, never trouble yourself about who is listening.

15. Always play as if a master heard you.

16. If any one lays a composition before you for the first time, for you to play, first read it over.

17. Have you done your musical day's work, and do you feel exhausted? Then do not constrain yourself to further labor. Better rest than work without joy or freshness.

18. Play nothing, as you grow older, which is merely *fashionable*. Time is precious. One must have a hundred lives, if he would acquaint himself only with all that is good.

19. Children cannot be brought up on sweetmeats and confectionery to be sound and healthy men. As the physical, so must the mental food be simple and nourishing. The masters have provided amply for the latter; keep to that.

20. A player may be very glib with finger-passages; they all in time grow commonplace and must be changed. Only where such facility serves higher ends, is it of any worth.

21. You must not give currency to poor compositions; on the contrary, you must do all you can to suppress them.

22. You should neither play poor compositions, nor even listen to them, if you are not obliged to.

23. Never try to acquire facility in what is called *Bravura*. Try in a composition to bring out the impression which the composer had in his mind; more than this attempt not; more than this is caricature.

24. Consider it a monstrosity to alter, or leave out anything, or to introduce any new-fangled ornaments in pieces by a good composer. That is the greatest outrage you can do to Art.

25. In the selection of your pieces for study, ask advice of older players; that will save you much time.

26. You must gradually make acquaintance with all the more important works of all the important masters.

27. Be not led astray by the brilliant popularity of the so-called great *virtuosi*.   Think more of the applause of artists than of that of the multitude.

28. Every fashion grows *unfashionable* again; if you persist in it for years, you find yourself a ridiculous coxcomb in the eyes of everybody.

29. It is more injury than profit to you to play a great deal before company.   Have a regard to other people ; but never play anything which, in your inmost soul, you are ashamed of.

30. Omit no opportunity, however, to play *with* others, in Duos, Trios, etc.   It makes your playing fluent, spirited, and easy.   Accompany a singer when you can.

31. If all would play first violin, we could get no orchestra together. Respect each musician, therefore, in his place.

32. Love your instrument, but do not have the vanity to think it the highest and only one.   Consider that there are others quite as fine. Remember, too, that there are singers, that the highest manifestations in Music are through chorus and orchestra combined.

33. As you progress, have more to do with scores than with *virtuosi*.

34. Practise industriously the Fugues of good masters, above all those of JOHN SEBASTIAN BACH.   Make the "Well-tempered Clavichord" your daily bread.   Then you will surely be a thorough musician.

35. Seek for your associates among those who know more than you.

36. For recreation from your musical studies, read the poets frequently.   Walk also in the open air !

37. Much may be learned from singers, male and female; but do not believe in them for everything.

38. Behind the mountains there live people, too.   Be modest; as yet you have discovered and thought nothing which others have not thought and discovered before you.   And even if you have done so, regard it as a gift from above, which you must share with others.

39. The study of the history of Music, supported by the actual hearing of the master compositions of the different epochs, is the shortest way to cure you of self-esteem and vanity.

40. A fine book on music is THIBAUT *Ueber Reinheit der Tonkunst* ("On Purity in the Musical Art").   Read it often as you grow older.

41. If you pass a church and hear the organ playing, go in and listen.   If it happens that you can occupy the organist's seat yourself, try your little fingers, and be amazed before this omnipotence of Music.

42. Improve every opportunity of practising upon the organ; there is no instrument which takes such speedy revenge on the impure and the slovenly in composition, or in playing, as the organ.

43. Sing frequently in choruses, especially on the middle parts. This makes you *musical*.

44. What is it to be *musical?* You are not so, if, with eyes fastened anxiously upon the notes, you play a piece through painfully to the end. You are not so, if, when some one turns over two pages at once, you stick and cannot go on. But you are musical, if, in a new piece, you anticipate pretty nearly what is coming, and in an old piece, know it by heart; in a word, if you have music, not in your fingers only, but in your head and heart.

45. But how does one become *musical?* Dear child, the main thing, a sharp ear, and a quick power of comprehension, comes, as in all things, from above. But the talent may be improved and elevated. You will become so, not by shutting yourself up all day like a hermit, practising mechanical studies; but by living, many-sided musical intercourse; and especially by constant familiarity with orchestra and chorus.

46. Acquire in season a clear notion of the compass of the human voice in its four principal classes; listen to it particularly in the chorus; ascertain in what interval its highest power lies, and in what other intervals it is best adapted to the expression of what is soft and tender.

47. Listen attentively to all Songs of the People; they are a mine of the most beautiful melodies, and open for you glimpses into the character of different nations.

48. Exercise yourself early in reading music in the old cleffs. Otherwise, many treasures of the past will remain locked against you.

49. Reflect early on the tone and character of different instruments: try to impress the peculiar *coloring* of each upon your ear.

50. Do not neglect to hear good Operas.

51. Reverence the Old, but meet the New also with a warm heart. Cherish no prejudice against names unknown to you.

52. Do not judge of a composition on a first hearing; what pleases you in the first moment is not always the best. Masters would be studied. Much will become clear to you for the first time in your old age.

53. In judging of compositions, distinguish whether they belong to the artistic category, or only aim at dilettantish entertainment. Stand up for those of the first sort; but do not worry yourself about the others!

54. "Melody" is the watchword of the Dilettanti, and certainly there is no music without melody. But understand well what they mean by it; nothing passes for a melody with them, but one that is easily comprehended or rhythmically pleasing. But there are other

melodies of a different stamp; open a volume of Bach, Mozart, or Beethoven, and you see them in a thousand various styles.   *   *
*   *   *   *   *   *   *   *   *   *   *   *

55. If you can find out little melodies for yourself on the piano, it is all very well. But if they come of themselves, when you are not at the piano, then you have still greater reason to rejoice, for then the inner sense of music is astir in you. The fingers must make what the head wills, not *vice versâ*.

56. If you begin to compose, make it all in your head. When you have got a piece all ready, then try it on the instrument. If your music came from your inmost soul, if *you* have felt it, then it will take effect on others.

57. If Heaven has bestowed on you a lively imagination, you will often sit in solitary hours spellbound to your piano, seeking expression for your inmost soul in harmonies; and all the more mysteriously will you feel drawn into magic circles, as it were, the more unclear the realm of harmony as yet may be to you. The happiest hours of youth are these. Beware, however, of abandoning yourself too often to a talent which may tempt you to waste power and time on phantoms. Mastery of form, the power of clearly moulding your productions, you will only gain through the sure token of writing. Write, then, more than you improvise.

58. Acquire an early knowledge of *directing;* watch good directors closely, and form a habit of directing *with* them, silently, and to yourself. This brings clearness.

59. Look about you well in life, as also in the other arts and sciences.

60. The Moral Laws are also those of Art.

61. By industry and perseverance you will always carry it higher.

62. From a pound of iron, bought for a few pence, many thousand watch-springs may be made, whereby the value is increased a hundred thousand fold. The pound which God has given you, improve it faithfully.

63. Without enthusiasm nothing real comes of Art.

64. Art is not for the end of getting riches. Only become a greater and greater Artist; the rest will come of itself.

65. Only when the form is entirely clear to you, will the spirit become clear.

66. Perhaps only genius understands genius fully.

67. Some one maintained, that a perfect musician must be able, on the first hearing of a complicated orchestral work, to see it as in bodily score before him. That is the highest that can be conceived of.

68. There is no end of learning.

CHAPTER XXX.

LETTERS ON THE ART OF PLAYING THE PIANO-FORTE.

By CARL CZERNY.

LETTER I.

First Rudiments of the Piano.

WHEN I, some years ago, had the pleasure of being personally acquainted with your family, I discovered in you so decided a talent for music, that I am rejoiced to hear you are now really about to devote yourself to the delightful art of playing the piano-forte. Your memory, at that time, easily retained any agreeable melody which you heard ; you manifested a natural feeling for time and musical expression ; and, added to this, your fingers and hands possessed all the natural qualities so necessary for playing the piano-forte—flexibility, quickness of movement, and lightness, without being either too weak or too stiff.

So decided a disposition and inclination for this fine art could not, in truth, remain long dormant ; for no art is more noble, nor more surely indicative of general mental cultivation, than music. By it we can command, not only for one's self, but for many others, a dignified and appropriate amusement ; and, where great progress has been made, we also insure a degree of distinction in the world, which is as agreeable to the amateur as to the professional artist.

The first principles, namely, a knowledge of the keys and the notes, are the only really tedious and unpleasant points in learning music. When you have once conquered them, you will every day experience more and more delight in continuing your studies.

Consider the matter as if you were for a time compelled to wend your way among somewhat tangled and thorny bushes, in order to arrive at last at a charming prospect, and a spot always blooming in vernal beauty.

The best remedy against this disagreeable necessity is, to endeavor to fix these preliminary subjects on your memory as firmly and quickly as possible. Such pupils as manifest, from the very outset, a desire and love for the thing, and who strongly and rationally apply their memories to the matter, will acquire a perfect knowledge of the keys and notes in a few weeks ; while others, frightened at the apparent tediousness of the acquisition, often lose several months in attaining the same object. Which, then, of these two ways is the better ?

Before anything else, I earnestly entreat you to acquire a graceful and appropriate position when sitting at the piano-forte. The seat which you use must be just so high that the elbows, when hanging down freely, may be a very little less elevated than the upper surface of the keys; and if your feet should not reach the ground, have a dwarf stool or ottoman made of a proper height to place them upon. You must always seat yourself exactly facing the middle of the key-board, and at such a distance from it that the tips of the elbows may be a little nearer to the keys than the shoulders.

Equally important is a graceful position and carriage of the head and upper part of the chest; it must neither be stiff nor bent.

It is not merely that an awkward position is disagreeable and ridiculous, but it also impedes, if not prevents, the development of a free and elegant style of playing.

The fore part of the arm (from the elbow to the fingers) should form a perfectly straight horizontal line; for the hand must neither rise upwards like a ball, nor be bent so as to slope downwards.

The fingers are to be so bent that the tips of them, together with that of the thumb, when extended outwards, may form one right line, and so that the keys may always be struck with the soft and fleshy tips of the fingers, and that neither the nails nor the flat surface of the fingers shall touch the keys. In striking the black keys, the fingers must be stretched out a little more; but even in this case they must always remain sufficiently bent.

The percussion on the keys is effected solely by the fingers, which, without any actual blow, must press each key firmly down; and in doing this, neither the hand nor the arm must be allowed to make any unnecessary movements. The thumb should always strike the key with its external narrow surface, and, in so doing, it must be but very little bent.

The white keys are to be struck on the middle of their anterior broad surfaces, and the black keys pretty close to their nearest extremities or ends.

You must take great care that you do not strike any key sideways or obliquely, as otherwise a contiguous and wrong key may chance to be touched; and, in music, nothing is worse than *producing wrong tones.*

While one finger strikes, the other fingers must be kept close to the keys, but always bent, and poised quite freely in the air; for we must not touch any key before the moment in which it is to be struck.

The most important of the fingers is the *thumb;* it must never be allowed to hang down below the key-board, but, on the contrary, it should always be held *over* the keys in such a way that its tip may be elevated a little higher than the upper surface of the black keys; and it must strike from this position.

To observe all these rules exactly, it is requisite that the elbows should never be too distant from the body, and that the arms, from the shoulder downwards, should hang freely, without being pressed against the body.

The knowledge of the notes is a mere affair of memory; and for every note, you must endeavor to find and strike the proper key, on the instant and without the least hesitation. In music this constitutes what is called *reading the notes;* and when you shall have acquired this readiness, you will have overcome the most difficult thing which elementary objects in music will be likely to present to you.

At first you will naturally learn only the notes in the treble clef, and for this purpose we may employ the following means:

First. When you look at a note, you must name it aloud, and then seek for and strike the key which belongs to it.

Secondly. When you strike at hazard any white key on the treble side of the key-board, you must name it aloud, and seek directly for the note belonging to it.

Thirdly. After having struck any white key at hazard, you must describe aloud, in words, what line or what space represents it.

Fourthly. You must often play through, slowly, some of the easiest pieces for beginners, note by note, and with great attention, naming each note as you proceed.

Fifthly. I must also recommend you to adopt the following expedient: since you are already much advanced in writing, you must learn to write music. The little trouble that this will cost, you will find amply recompensed by great advantages. Notes are much easier to write than letters; and, if you daily devote a quarter of an hour to this task, in a couple of weeks you will become sufficiently expert at it.

Your teacher will give you the instructions requisite for this purpose; and when you have been in this way accustomed to place the notes as they come, exactly on or between the lines, copy out daily one of the easiest elementary lessons, and then write in letters over each note its proper denomination; after which, play the piece over slowly.

When, in this way, you have learned to know perfectly all the degrees in the treble clef, and are able to play slowly, but correctly, with both hands, little pieces in the treble clef, then take the bass notes, and proceed with them just in the same manner.

You must practise each piece, paying the strictest attention to the fingering indicated, till you are able to execute it without stopping or stumbling. Each day you should read through a couple of fresh little pieces, to accustom the eye and the fingers to the various and ever new passages which are formed by means of the notes.

At first, after each note, we must also look at the key which is to be struck; but afterwards, when we have attained a tolerable certainty in finding the keys, it is better to fix the eye on the notes rather than on the keys.

And now allow me in this letter to offer this last very important remark: the best knowledge of the notes avails us very little, if, *at the same time*, the fingers do not begin to develop that degree of flexibility which is requisite for striking the keys, and for playing in general. I, therefore, most earnestly recommend you to practise daily, with untiring diligence and the greatest attention, five-finger exercises in both hands, which your instructor will explain to you, in order that your fingers may speedily acquire that pliability, independence, and volubility which are absolutely necessary to playing.

Do not be alarmed at the little trouble and application that this may require; try three or four times every day, for at least a quarter of an hour each time, to play through the exercises with attention. In fact, it is as impossible to play the piano-forte well with stiff and untractable fingers, as to dance well with stiff and untractable feet. *Volubility of finger is one of the chief requisites in piano-forte playing.*

It is very proper that your teacher gives you an hour's lesson every day. If, in addition to this, you daily dedicate another hour—or, if possible, two hours—to practising by yourself, you will in a few months have forever conquered all that is difficult or tedious in the elementary branches of playing; and you will each day see augmented the pleasure which the delightful art of music so richly bestows on its votaries.

LETTER II.

TWO MONTHS LATER.

On Touch, Tone, and the Mode of Treating the Piano-forte.

I HAVE just received your welcome letter, and learn from it that you have already made considerable progress in reading the letters, and that you are able to play several of the first and easiest little pieces, somewhat slowly, perhaps, but still intelligibly.

Continue daily to decipher a couple of new little pieces, and at the same time to practise still more those which you have already learned, so that these latter ones may go off quicker and quicker, and that you may each week study at least two fresh pieces. For, as you have an earnest wish to attain to a high degree of excellence in piano-forte playing, you must look upon all that has been given to you as yet only as a *means to that end*, and, indeed, as that means which will conduct to this end *as quickly and as agreeably as possible.*

I could not refrain from laughing a little, if I may be allowed to tell you so, at your complaining to me how much your master vexed and tormented you with finger exercises, with rules relating to touch, to the position of the hands, to clearness, volubility, etc.

"Ah!" you exclaim, in a manner quite touching, "must all this really be so?"

Yes, such is indeed the case; and here I cannot assist you. Your teacher is quite right in being so strict as to all these points, and I will explain the reason why. From every musical instrument we may produce either a fine tone or a detestable one, *according as we handle it.* The same excellent violin which, in the hands of a clever player, sounds so delightfully, will, when handled by a clumsy person, yield disagreeable sounds. It is the same with the piano-forte. If it is not properly handled by the player, or if we merely thump and bang the keys, the best instrument will sound hard and unpleasant. On the other hand, if we employ too little force, or do not know how to use this power in a proper manner, the tone will be poor and dull, and the performance unintelligible, and without soul or expression.

The interior mechanism of the keys is such that the strings will only sound well when we

First. Strike each key perpendicularly; that is, straight downwards, and exactly in the middle, and therefore not sideways nor obliquely.

Secondly. When, after the percussion, each key is so firmly pressed down as to cause the full tone of the instrument to be audible.

Thirdly. When, before the percussion, we do not raise the finger too high; as, otherwise, along with the tone there will be heard the blow on the key.

Fourthly. When the hand and arm, even when striking with considerable force, do not make any jumping, chopping, or oscillating movement; for you will find that the fingers cannot possibly play pleasantly and tranquilly when the hands and arms are unsteady.

Fifthly and Lastly. When the player observes all these rules in rapid runs, or even in skips and extensions, as strictly as in slow and quiet passages.

All the finger exercises, and particularly the *scales*, have no other end than to accustom the fingers to the application of these rules so thoroughly, that the player shall practise all that he studies in future strictly according to the principles we have given.

"*Ah! the scales,*" you write to me; "*that* is truly a tedious story! Are these things, then, really as necessary as my teacher says?*"

Yes, these scales are the *most necessary point of all,* not only for beginners, but even for pupils who are much advanced; and, indeed, the most expert players do and must constantly have recourse to and practise them. Permit me to demonstrate this to you, as I know that you have a good understanding, and are fond of reflecting.

You know already that the passing of the thumb *under* the other fingers, and of the three middle fingers *over* the thumb, is absolutely necessary, and that it is the only means by which we are enabled to strike a long series of keys quickly one after the other.

But this passing of the thumb and fingers, even in the most rapid passages, must be effected in a manner so natural, equal, and unlabored, that the hearer shall not be able to distinguish the smallest interruption or inequality. This, however, is almost the greatest difficulty in piano-forte playing; and it is possible only when neither the arm nor the hand makes the smallest movement upwards or sideways, and when the joints of all the fingers attain gradually and by long practice so great a degree of flexibility and address, that in a rapid run over the key-board one is almost tempted to think that the player has at least fifty fingers on each hand. To attain this highly necessary property, there is no other means than the most diligent, uninterrupted daily practice of the scales in all the keys.

But these scales have many other various uses. There are few musical compositions in which they are not introduced by the author in some shape or other. In every piece, whether written to-day or one hundred years ago, they are the principal means by which every passage and every melody is formed. The diatonic scales or the chords broken into arpeggios, you will everywhere find employed innumerable times.

You will now easily imagine what an advantage it gives a player when he is perfectly acquainted, in all the keys, with these FUNDAMENTAL PASSAGES, from which so many others are derived; and what a command over the entire key-board, and what an easy insight into any musical piece, he gains thereby.

Further, no property is more necessary and important to the player than a well-developed *flexibility, lightness, and volubility* of the fingers. This cannot be acquired in any way so quickly as by the practice of the scales. For, if we were to try to attain those qualities by the merely studying of different musical compositions, we should spend whole years to accomplish our purpose. Many beautiful pieces require to be executed in a very quick degree of movement, and with great volubility of finger. But how tiresome and detestable would these same pieces sound, if played slow, stiff, and unequal! And even those compositions which are slow on the whole, still contain many occasional runs and embellishments which require great rapidity of finger. All these he has already conquered who is able to play the scales well and with sufficient quickness.

At present you cannot form an idea of the beauty and effect which is produced by a pure, clear, rapid, and *strictly equal* execution of such runs; they are musical rows of pearls, and many great artists are more particularly distinguished on account of their peculiar excellence in the performance of them. You will no doubt have already remarked that correct *fingering* is a very important part of piano-forte playing, and one which costs every pupil a good deal of labor. Now, the scales contain all the principal rules of fingering, and they are in themselves sufficient, in almost all cases, to show the pupil the right path. What do you say to all these advantages? Is it not well worth the while to occupy yourself seriously with these same tiresome scales?

I must now tell you in *what way* you ought to proceed to do this, for, if *studied in a wrong manner*, the scales may prove as injurious as they are capable of being serviceable when properly practised. You know that the five fingers are by no means equal to each other in natural strength. Thus, for example, the thumb is much stronger than any of the other fingers; the first finger is much stronger than the little finger; and the third finger, on the contrary, is, with almost every person, the weakest of all. The *pianist*, however, must know how to employ these various degrees of power, so that in playing the scales all the fingers may strike their appropriate keys *with perfect equality of strength;* for the scales sound well only when they are played in every respect *with the most exact equality.*

This equality is *threefold,* namely:

First. Equality of strength.

No one note ought to sound in the smallest degree louder than another, whether it be struck with the thumb, or the first, second, third, or little finger.

Second. Equality in point of quickness.

Each note must follow the preceding one strictly in the same degree of movement, whether we play the scales slow or quick.

Thirdly and Lastly. Equality in holding the keys down.

No key must be held down for a longer or shorter time than the rest; that is, each finger must only keep its key pressed down till the following one is struck, and it must then be taken up exactly at the very instant that the next finger comes in contact with its key. This must, of course, also be observed in *passing the thumb under* the middle fingers, or in passing the latter *over* the thumb.

If we offend even against only *one* of these three principal rules, the equality and beauty of the run are destroyed, and the utility of the practice lost. Each scale, therefore, must be practised, first with the right hand only, and then with both hands, and, at first, *extremely slow,* always consulting the judgment of your teacher, or taking the counsel of your own good ear, as to whether the fingers sufficiently observe all the rules.

From week to week you must increase the degree of rapidity, till at last all the fingers are in a condition to fly over the keys with lightness, firmness, and distinct and beautiful execution. Every day, when you seat yourself at the piano-forte, let the *scales* be, for one-half hour, the first thing which you attack; as by this means the fingers will be got in readiness for everything else.

LETTER III.

TWO MONTHS LATER.

On Time, Subdivision of the Notes, and Fingering.

THE intelligence of your further progress rejoiced me very much. Your fingers already begin to develop a well-regulated flexibility; your touch and execution are no longer heavy and sluggish; the finger exercises, the runs, and scale passages go off tolerably quick, light, and equal; and lastly, you already play several dozen little pieces without faults, and generally without stumbling. You see that a reasonable degree of diligence and obedience to the precepts of your teacher will soon be rewarded by the most pleasing results.

The difficulty which the observance of the ♯, ♮, ♭, ✕, and ♭♭ still causes you, will soon disappear, if you firmly apply your memory to this point, and if you constantly take good notice of, and learn to quickly retain, the marks of transposition which are indicated at the beginning of each piece, as well as those which occur accidentally in the measure.

But the time and the *subdivision of the notes* cause you much trouble, and we will therefore treat a little on this subject to-day.

The *subdivision of the notes* in music is a thing so certain and so positively determined, that we cannot well commit a fault against it, *if we give to each note and rest its exact value, and if, in so doing, we consult the eye rather than the ear.* For the eye always sees aright when it is supported by the memory; but the ear by itself may very often be deceived, particularly in beginners.

The duration of the notes is, as you know, expressed by the fingers being *held down* on the keys; that of the rests, on the contrary, by the fingers *being kept off the keys, and free;* and we must take care not to confound these two things, for each note must be held exactly as long as its prescribed value requires, and the key must not be quitted either sooner or later. Simple and easy as this rule appears, it is often sinned against by much better players than yourself. This arises from the circumstance that most persons are neglectful on this head when they are first taught; partly out of carelessness, and partly also because the holding down of the keys appears tiresome and inconvenient, or, on the contrary, sometimes because the fingers are too unapt and sluggish to quit the keys at the right moment.

Those who hold down the keys *too long,* accustom themselves to a lingering, adhesive, indistinct, and often discordant manner of playing. Those who quit the keys *too soon,* fall into an unconnected, broken style of playing, which is without melody, and which at last degenerates into mere hacking and thumping the keys. That both modes will conduct us into the wrong path I need not further explain to you.

The art of subdividing the notes consists in introducing the quicker notes, exactly at the right moment, among the longer ones.

But, as groups of notes occasionally occur which must be played *very quick,* if we are to observe the exact movement and the length of the measure, you will see how necessary it is that the fingers should early be accustomed to play with readiness and rapidity. For without this, even with the best knowledge of the subdivision of notes, we are at every moment in danger either of lagging behind in the time, or of scrambling over these quicker notes in any way we best can.

You perceive here, again, that the diligent practice of finger exercises and scales is of the highest importance ; for the quick *perception* of the different values of the notes requires only a *practised eye*, while for the rapid and correct *execution of them*, we also require a well-practised finger.

It is of great advantage to you that in every piece your teacher either counts aloud each separate measure, or beats the time with a pencil or bit of stick, by which you are compelled to continue always in the right time.

Equally useful is it, that you have already studied several easy pieces as duets for four hands, occasionally playing the lower or bass part.

The two following capital points are most essential, and must not be overlooked :

First. Strictness in taking the right keys.

For false letters produce intervals which generally sound very disagreeably, and strike as unpleasantly on the ear as a spot of ink on a white frock does on the eye.

Secondly. Correctness in keeping time.

For, without time, music is unintelligible, and lost on the hearer.

To *correctness in playing* belong attention, tranquillity, a good position of the hands, correct fingering, and the requisite habit of striking every key in the middle of its breadth, so as not to touch any contiguous key.

To *keeping time* belong also the following points :

At the first deciphering of a new musical piece, the beginner cannot, of course, easily play in time, since he must bestow great attention on *taking the notes correctly*, and on the fingering, and must stop at each wrong taken key to set himself right. As soon, however, as this is amended, he must endeavor to play through the piece ; at first slowly, indeed, and then continue to practise it, till he can go through it as quickly as the composer has indicated.

If you can accustom yourself, while playing, to count *aloud*, it will be exceedingly advantageous to you. Beating the time with the foot cannot well be recommended, because it often settles into a bad habit.

When long rests occur in both hands, counting mentally or aloud is exceedingly necessary ; for you know that, in every musical composition, each measure must occupy exactly the same portion of time as the others, whether it consists of notes or rests.

Hitherto I have only spoken of that sort of keeping time in which we neither come to a stand-still, nor omit, nor pass over anything. But there is another sort of keeping time, in which we may observe all this very correctly, and yet commit errors against time.

These faults consist in this—that, in the course of the piece, we either continually play *quicker and quicker*, or *slower and slower ;* or else, that we sometimes play too quick, and then again too slow.

Into the error of *accelerating* the time, just such young and lively persons as yourself are most apt to fall ; and who knows whether I have not guessed right when I imagine that you sometimes begin a piece which goes off pretty fluently, at first very quietly and sagely ; but then, becoming excited as you go on, you play quicker and quicker, and, at last, finish with such rapidity as if your fingers were holding a runaway pony? Have I not guessed rightly?

To avoid this, you must practise even those pieces *which you already play well*, as composedly and as attentively as when you first began to study them; and in so doing, you must not allow the fingers to indulge their own fancies, or to be in the least degree inattentive.

The opposite fault of *hanging back*, or dragging in the time, generally proceeds from our having begun too fast; and by that means stumbling against difficulties which we cannot overcome in that quick degree of movement.

Hence this capital rule: *never begin a piece quicker than you can with certainty go on with it to the very end.* There are exceptions to this rule, which you will be taught by and by, when you learn the higher branches of expression and execution.

You will already have remarked how necessary correct fingering is in playing. A single ill-chosen finger may often cause the complete failure of a whole passage, or at least make it sound coarse, unequal, and disagreeable. As doubtless you have studied all the elementary pieces exactly with the fingering indicated, your fingers are, to a certain degree, already accustomed to a regular system of fingering. But as, in other compositions, you may, by and by, be often in doubt on this head, I will impart a few rules on this subject, as to what must be *observed* or *avoided* in every regular system of fingering.

First. When several keys are to be played one after another, either in ascending or in descending, and five fingers are not sufficient for this purpose, the four longer fingers must never be turned over one another; but we must either pass the thumb *under*, or pass the three middle fingers *over* the thumb.

Secondly. The thumb must never be placed on the black keys.

Thirdly. We must not strike two or more keys one after another with the self-same finger; for each key must always retain its own finger.

Fourthly. In runs, the little finger should never be placed on the black keys.

Fifthly. In chords and wide extensions, however, the thumb, as well as the little finger, may occasionally fall upon the black keys.

Sixthly. The fingering given for the *scales* must be resorted to everywhere, and as much as possible.

Seventhly. At each note that we strike, we must consider whether, for the following notes, the appropriate fingers stand in readiness.

In general, that mode of fingering must be chosen by which we may most easily and naturally be able to maintain a tranquil and fine position of the hands, a firm and perpendicular percussion, as well as a correct holding down of the keys, and a beautiful and connected performance of the melody and of the scales and runs.

I am so convinced that an exact observance of what I have hitherto laid down will, in a short time, enable you to conquer all elementary difficulties, that I trust, in my next intelligence from you, to receive the assurance of this being the case.

LETTER IV.

On Expression, and Graces or Embellishments.

HAVE I not already told you that the zealous practice of all the finger exercises, and the quickly studying of a good many musical pieces, would soon bring you very forward? You write me that your fingers have already acquired very considerable facility and certainty; that you now begin to study pieces of more importance, development, and difficulty; that you are already able to play, at sight, many short, easy movements, intelligibly and without stopping; and that even keys with a good many sharps or flats do not easily confuse you.

You are now arrived at the epoch where the art begins to proffer you true, noble, and intellectual pleasures, and in which the new and continually more and more beautiful compositions with which you will now become acquainted, will give you an idea of the inexhaustible riches and variety in music.

But do not neglect to still continue practising, with equal or even greater zeal, the finger exercises, and especially the **scales** in all the keys.

The utility of this accessory practice is infinite; and, in particular, the diatonic and chromatic scales possess peculiar properties, which even the most skilful players have yet to fathom. I also request you most earnestly, while you are studying new pieces, not by any means to forget those already learned, not even the earliest ones.

New pieces serve but little if, on their account, the preceding ones are forgotten.

For the adroitness and expertness of the fingers, the eyes and the ears must of necessity repose firmly and fundamentally on the experience which we have already gained; while these qualities are to be enlarged and refined by new acquisitions. If, for example, you forget a piece which it took you three weeks to learn, these three weeks are as good as lost. You should therefore retain, as a sort of absolute property, all the pieces you have ever learned; keep them safely, and never lend or give them away.

"Yes," you say, "if it did not take up so much time to continue practising what I have already learned, and also to study new pieces."

You cannot imagine what may be effected in one single day, if we *properly avail ourselves of the time.*

If, with a fixed determination to excel on the piano-forte, you dedicate to it, *daily, only three hours,* of which about half an hour shall be appropriated to the exercises, as much more to playing over the old pieces, and the remaining time to the study of new compositions, this will assuredly enable you, by degrees, to attain a very commanding degree of excellence, without necessarily obliging you to neglect your other pursuits.

Your instructor has already accustomed you to observe, in general, the marks of expression; as, *forte, piano, legato, staccato,* etc. The more you begin to overcome all the mechanical difficulties of piano-forte playing, the greater attention you must give to this important subject—*expression.*

Expression, feeling, and sensibility are the soul of music, as of every other art. If we were to play a piece of music with exactly the same degree of forte or piano throughout, it would sound as ridiculous as if we were to recite a beautiful poem in the same monotonous tone in which we are used to repeat the multiplication table.

In every composition, the marks of expression, *f.*, *p.*, *cres.*, *dim.*, *legato*, *staccato*, *acceler.*, *ritard.*, etc., are so exactly indicated by the composer, that the performer can never be in doubt where he is to play loud or soft, increasing or decreasing as to tone, connected or detached, hurrying onwards in the time, or holding it back.

The same exactitude with which you are obliged to observe the notes, the marks of transposition, the fingering, and the time, you must likewise employ with regard to the marks of expression.

But the most difficult part of the business is *always to observe the proper medium* at each mark of expression; for you already know that there is great diversity in the shades and degrees of *forte*, *piano*, *legato*, *staccato*, *accelerando*, and *ritardando*.

The utmost fortissimo should never degenerate into mere hammering and thumping, or into maltreating the instrument.

Similarly, the most gentle pianissimo ought never to become indistinct and unintelligible.

You possess an excellent piano-forte, by one of our best makers; and you will already have remarked that the most gentle pressure of the finger on a key produces a perceptible alteration and modification in the tone; and that we may play with great power, without any excessive exertion, and without using any unnecessary and ridiculous movements of the hands, arms, shoulders, or head. For, unhappily, many, even very good pianists, are guilty of these and similar contortions and grimaces, against which I must warn you.

Many, too, have the detestable habit, when they wish to strike a note with peculiar emphasis, of elevating their knuckles so much that the hand seems to form waves, like troubled waters.

Others endeavor to manifest their feelings by widely jerking out their elbows; or they mark the commencement of every measure by making a low bow with their head and chest, as if they were desirous of showing reverence to their own playing. Others, after every short note, suddenly take up their hands as far from the keys as if they had touched a red-hot iron. Many, while playing, put on a fierce and crabbed countenance; others, again, assume a perpetual simper, etc. One of the worst faults is carrying to excess the ritardando and accelerando, so that we are often several minutes without knowing whether the piece is written in triple or in double time. This produces nearly the same effect as if some one were addressing us in a strange, unintelligible language.

To all these faults we may accustom ourselves, in the zeal of practice, *without knowing it;* and when, to our mortification, we are made to observe them, it is often too late wholly to leave them off.

Do not suppose, however, that you are to sit at the piano as stiff and cold as a wooden doll. Some graceful movements are *necessary* while playing; it is only the *excess* that must be avoided.

When we have to play in the highest or lowest octave, a gentle inclination of the body is at once necessary and appropriate. When we have to play difficult passages, chords struck loud and short, or skips, the hands are and must be allowed a moderate degree of movement. As we must sometimes look at the notes, and sometimes at the hands, a slight movement of the head is, if not necessary, at least very excusable. Still, however, you should accustom yourself to look rather at the notes than at the fingers.

But the elegant deportment of polished life must always be transferred to the art; and the rule applies generally, "that every movement which conduces really and essentially to our better playing is allowed;" here, however, we must avoid all that is unnecessary and superfluous.

At present it would be too early to direct your attention to certain more refined rules of expression. In the meantime I beg of you to observe, in the strictest manner, all that each composer has indicated on this head in his works; and to try to execute each piece in a pure and flowing manner, and in the time indicated by the author. Towards effecting this last object, Maelzel's metronome will afford you very great assistance in most modern compositions.

The *graces*—namely, the trill, the turn, the appoggiatura, etc.—are the flowers of music; and the clear, correct, and delicate execution of them, embellishes and exalts every melody and every passage. But when they are played stiff, hard, or unintelligibly, they may rather be compared to blots of ink or spots of dirt.

The trill is peculiarly important; and to a pianist, the elegant, equal, and rapid execution of it is as much an ornament and a duty as the equal and pearly execution of the scales. In the right hand, at least, it ought to be played alike well *with all the fingers*. The equality of the trill can only be attained by lifting up both fingers to an *equal height*, and striking the keys with equal force. You ought to devote a few minutes daily to this particular practice.

LETTER V.

TWO MONTHS LATER.

On the Keys, on Studying a Piece, and on Playing in the Presence of Others.

You are now well acquainted with all the twenty-four keys, and with the scales and chords belonging to them, and it is with pleasure I learn that you even now daily play through all the scales and passages in them as diligently as you formerly did those in the twelve major keys; and that you acknowledge the many advantages of these exercises, by which also you save yourself the labor of wading through so many tedious *études*, or professed studies.

One of the most necessary acquirements for a pianist is to be *equally practised and ready in all the keys*. There are many who are as much startled at a piece having four or five sharps or flats for its signature as though they saw a spectre. And, nevertheless, to the *fingers* all keys are in reality of equal difficulty; for there are as difficult compositions in C major as in C sharp major. Only that the *eye* and the *memory* must be early accustomed to this great number of marks of transposition.

As, in such unusual keys, the black keys must be principally employed, and as they are narrower than the white ones, and therefore less certain as to the striking of them; it is absolutely requisite, on the part of the player, that he should keep his hand particularly firm, and somewhat higher than usual over the keys, and employ a very decided touch, in order to acquire the same degree of certainty as on the white keys.

You complain that the studying of difficult pieces still costs you much time and labor. There is a certain remedy against this, which I may call the *art of studying*, and which I impart to you, as far as it can be done in writing.

There are pupils who study such compositions attentively enough, it is true, but so slowly, and with such frequent interruptions, that these pieces become tedious and disagreeable to them before they have half learned them. Such pupils often take half a year to learn a few pieces tolerably; and by this wasteful expenditure of time always remain in the background.

Others, on the contrary, try to conquer everything by force; and imagine that they shall succeed in this by practising for hours, laboriously indeed, but in an inattentive and thoughtless manner, and by hastily playing over all kinds of difficulties innumerable times. These persons play till their fingers are lamed; but how? confusedly, over-hastily, and without expression; or, what is still worse, *with a false expression.*

We may escape all this by keeping the right medium between these two ways. When, therefore, you begin to learn a new and somewhat difficult piece, you must devote the first hours to deciphering the notes strictly and correctly in a slow time. You must also fix upon the fingering to be employed, and gain a general insight over the whole. This, in a single piece, can at most require but a few days. Then the whole piece must be played over quietly and composedly, but at the same time attentively, and without any distraction of ideas, till we are enabled to execute it without trouble, and in the exact time indicated by the author.

Single passages of great difficulty may be practised apart. Still, however, they ought to be often repeated in connection with the rest of the piece.

All this, too, may be completed in a few days. But now begins the time when we must also learn to *play it with beauty and elegance.*

Now all the marks of expression must be observed with redoubled attention; and we must endeavor to seize correctly on the character of the composition, and to enforce it in our performance according to its total effect.

To this belongs the very important quality, *that the player should know how to listen properly to himself, and to judge of his own performance with accuracy.* He who does not possess this gift, is apt, in practising alone, to spoil all that he has acquired correctly in the presence of his teacher.

But I must once more remind you that we can only study new pieces quickly and well when we have not forgotten those already learned. There are, alas! many pupils who play only that piece well which they have just been taught. All those acquired before are neglected and thrown aside. Such pupils will never make any great progress. For you must own that those persons who play fifty pieces well are much more clever than those who, like a bird organ, can only play two or three pieces in a tolerable manner; and that the first, by a proper employment of our time, is very possible, I believe I have already said to you.

Your teacher has acted very properly in early accustoming you to play occasionally before others. At first this, as you write me, was very disagreeable to you, and you felt much frightened in so doing. "But now," say you, "I think nothing of it; nay, it generally gives me great pleasure, particularly when all goes off well." And there you are quite right. To what purpose do we learn, but to give pleasure, not only to ourselves, but also to our parents and friends? And assuredly there is no higher satisfaction than in being able to distinguish one's self before a large company, and in receiving an honorable acknowledgment of one's diligence and talent.

But, to bring matters to this point, we must be thoroughly sure of our business; for want of success is, on the contrary, as vexatious as tormenting and disgraceful· Above all, you must select, for this purpose, such compositions as are fully within your powers, and respecting the good effect of which you can entertain no doubt. Every difficult piece becomes doubly difficult when we play it before others, because the natural diffidence of the performer impedes the free development of his abilities.

Many half-formed players imagine that everything will be right, if they do but step forward at once with a difficult piece by some celebrated composer. But by this means they neither do honor to the composition nor to themselves, but merely expose themselves to the danger of exciting *ennui*, and, at best, of being applauded from politeness and compassion.

Many, otherwise very good players, have in this manner, by an unsuitable choice of pieces, lost both their musical reputation and all future confidence in themselves.

When playing before others, you should particularly endeavor to execute your *well-studied* piece with tranquillity and self-possession, without hurrying, without allowing your ideas to wander, and *more especially without coming to a stand-still;* for this last is the most unpleasant fault which we can commit before an audience.

Before you commence, the fingers must be kept quite warm; you must avoid any inconvenient mode of dress; and you should, if possible, always play on a piano-forte with which you are well acquainted; for an instrument, of which the touch is much lighter or much heavier than that which one is accustomed to, may very much confuse a player.

But it may often happen that you are suddenly required, in the company of intimate acquaintance, to play over some trifle to them.

It is very necessary, therefore, that you should study and commit to memory a number of easy but tasteful pieces, so that, on such occasions, you may be able to play them *by heart:* for it appears rather childish to be obliged, for every trifle, to turn over one's collection of music; or, when in a strange place, to be always obliged to draw back, with an excuse "that you cannot play anything by heart."

For this purpose, short rondos, pretty airs with variations, melodies from operas, nay, even dance tunes, waltzes, quadrilles, marches, etc., are perfectly suitable; for *everything does credit to the player which is well played.*

The playing before others has also the great advantage that it compels one to study with unusual zeal, for the idea that we must play before an audience, spurs us on to a much greater measure of diligence than if we play only to ourselves.

LETTER VI.

On the Selection of Compositions most Suitable for each Pianist.

In the choice of musical pieces, we should always bear in mind the following points:

First. That we ought always to proceed from the more easy to the more difficult as to execution.

Secondly. That, as far as possible, we should make ourselves acquainted with the works of *all* the great composers, and not by any means tie ourselves down to any favorite author.

Thirdly. That, by degrees, we should also thoroughly learn the classical and truly valuable works of the earlier composers.

Every distinguished composer requires to be played in a style peculiar to himself. With many, there predominates a brilliant, showy, and strongly marked manner; with others, an expressive, quiet, connected, and gentle style of playing is most generally called for; others, again, require a characteristic, impassioned, or even fantastic or humorous expression; and, in many compositions, a tender, warm, playful, and pleasing mode of execution is most suitable. Lastly, there are pieces which include all these different styles, and which therefore compel the player to adopt corresponding alterations of manner in his performance. Thus, for example, *Hummel's* compositions require an extraordinary and pearl-like mode of execution, which is produced by a lightly *dropping* of the keys. In *Beethoven's* works this style will seldom be suitable, as in them great characteristic energy, deep feeling, often capricious humor, and a sometimes very *legato*, and at others a very marked and emphatic, style of playing are requisite.

A piece which is played too fast or too slow loses all its effect and becomes quite disfigured. Where the time is not marked according to Maelzel's metronome, the player must look to the Italian words which indicate the degree of movement, as *allegro*, *moderato*, *presto*, etc., and likewise to the character of the composition, and gradually learn by experience to know their real significations.

No less important is the proper mode of treating the *pedals*. By a proper employment of the forte or damper pedal, the player is enabled to produce effects which would seem to require that he should have two pairs of hands at his command. But, used at an improper time, this pedal causes an unpleasant and unintelligible noise, which falls on the ear as disagreeably as writing on wet paper falls on the eye.

I have already explained how important to the pupil is a gradual and easy progression, as to difficulty, in the selection of pieces intended for him; and I shall now add a few words more on this head. Every composer, as well as every player, founds his art and his science on what his *predecessors* have already done; adding to that the inventions of his own talent. By these natural steps in advance, it is evident that the compositions of the present distinguished pianists are in many respects much more difficult than those of times gone by; and that whoever desires to study them must already possess great knowledge of music, and a very considerable degree of execution.

Many pupils, however, as soon as their fingers have acquired some little facility, are led astray by the charms of novelty, and run into the error of attacking the most difficult compositions. Not a few who can hardly play the scales in a decent manner, and who ought to practice for years *studies* and easy and appropriate pieces, have the presumption to attempt *Hummel's concertos* or *Thalberg's fantasias*.

The natural result of this over-haste is, that such players, by omitting the requisite preparatory studies, always continue imperfect, lose much time, and are at last unable to execute either difficult or easy pieces in a creditable manner.

This is the true cause why, although so many talented young persons devote themselves to the piano-forte, we are still not so over and above rich in good players, as, beyond all doubt, was the case formerly; and why so many, with the best dispositions, and often with enormous industry, still remain but mediocre and indifferent performers.

Many other pupils run into the error of attempting to decide on the merits of a composition before they are able to play it properly. From this it happens that many excellent pieces appear contemptible to them, while the fault lies in their playing them in a stumbling, incorrect, and unconnected manner, often coming to a stand-still on false and discordant harmonies, missing the time, etc.

You have no doubt frequently been placed in this situation, and, perhaps, you have sometimes impatiently thrown aside a piece which did not much promise to please you. In this manner you must, in the sequel, have often lost that exquisite enjoyment which the ingenious and elaborate works of the great masters offer to you, if you have the patience to overcome the difficulties generally inseparable from them.

Here more particularly belong compositions in what is called the *strict style;* as, for example, the works of *Handel, Bach,* and other masters of this stamp. For the execution of such pieces, generally written in several parts, and in the *fugue* style, and of such single passages in the same style as we often meet with in the most modern compositions, there are required a strict *legato,* and a very firm and equal touch; and also a clear enunciation of each single part; and for the attainment of all this, the employment of a peculiar mode of fingering, which, in general, deviates very much from the usual one, and which chiefly consists in quickly and adroitly substituting one finger for another on the same key, while it is held down, and without sounding it anew.

By this substitution, the five fingers are in a manner multiplied *ad infinitum,* and we are enabled to play each of the four parts, of which such passages in general consist, as smoothly, connectedly, and in as singing a manner as though we had so many hands.

Letters VII., VIII., IX., and X. are devoted to Thorough Bass and extemporaneous performance.

CHAPTER XXXI.

BURROWES' GUIDE TO PRACTICE.

INTRODUCTION.

THE course of practice recommended in the following remarks cannot be expected to coincide with the views of every instructor, or be equally applicable to all pupils; the point sought to be established is, that the pupil should have a regular system to go by, and in whatever particular this may differ from the views of the teacher upon the various points connected with the mode of practicing, he can easily point out the difference he wishes to be made; at all events, if this work serve no other purpose, it will have the effect of bringing the subject of practice more particularly into notice, and, in default of better instructions, be at least some guide to the pupil, and prevent much of that waste of time which daily occurs with those who, even with the greatest diligence, do not combine method. It may be said that every instructor is the best judge, and gives his own directions as to what and how his pupil shall practice. To a certain extent, this is true; but, upon the principle that "everybody's business is nobody's business," it may frequently be left undone; besides, if it be done, a master cannot constantly repeat the same thing, and pupils do sometimes forget.

No master disputes the utility of the daily practice of Exercises and Scales, but many pupils have a great disinclination thereto; and, though it is not to be doubted that every one will practice them to the extent he may be desired, still, as that which is done willingly, and with a conviction of its being conducive to improvement, will always be not only more pleasant, but much more satisfactory in its results, than that which is done as a mere task, the author assures all pupils that more improvement will be made in one month by those who practice them daily than will be made in six or even twelve months by those who do not.

The greatest performers never discontinue the practice of Scales and Exercises.

It is scarcely necessary to remark that practice, to be efficient, must be upon a good principle. Practice upon a bad principle, or, what is more common, without any principle at all, will but confirm error, and render it more difficult to conquer. It is, therefore, essential to prevent any bad habit from being acquired; and the very first time a child puts its fingers on the keys, it should be taught to do so in a proper manner. This opinion is much at variance with common practice, which is, to let a child learn *any how* at first, and, when it has

contracted all sorts of bad habits, to give it a good master, who has
not only to teach, but also to unteach, if, indeed, that can ever be
done. A child's learning anything may be compared to the winding
of a skein of thread, which, if it have never been tangled, may be
easily, though perhaps in some instances slowly, wound; but if it be
tangled, not only will the trouble be increased tenfold, but the chances
are that it will be broken in many places, and consequently never perfect. Some pupils have naturally, that is to say, without any instruction as to how it should be done, a better mode of touching the keys
than others, as some persons are naturally more or less graceful in all
they do, while others are more or less awkward; but it is not sufficient
that anything be well done; it must be done well upon principle.
Those who have what may be termed a natural good touch will have
less difficulty to contend with; but they must not be allowed to be
ignorant of the principle upon which they do well. It is not, however,
in the province of these remarks to give a detailed explanation of the
principle upon which different passages should be played. This can
only be properly and progressively done by a good instructor.

One thing cannot be too strongly impressed on the mind of the pupil,
which is the necessity of patience and perseverance in thoroughly understanding and playing correctly, though perhaps not fluently, the
early exercises, as upon these will depend all the future progress. If
there be but two notes to be played, still, those two notes must be well
done, and it is not sufficient that the pupil be able to do them well once
or twice, but he must practice doing so; and the rule for going forward
must never be when anything has been played a certain number of
times, or when it is merely correct, but when, by repetition, it has
become habitual to do it well. As an incitement to perseverance, it
may be remarked, that those who understand and do play even two
notes well may soon, with the same application, play four, and so on;
whereas those who pass over the first two notes, or anything else,
without being thoroughly understood and sufficiently practiced, will
never make any satisfactory progress.

For the sake of giving precise directions, it has been assumed that
every pupil should practice TWO HOURS A DAY; and it may be with
truth said, that those who expect to make any efficient progress should
do this at the least. Those who adhere strictly to the directions for
the two hours may, it is conceived, from the habits acquired thereby,
be safely left to their own discretion for any additional time.

ON PRACTICE IN GENERAL.

Fixed hours should be appointed for practice. It is not enough to
say that a pupil should practice two or more hours a day, but the time
for so doing should be fixed; every day's experience shows that whatever is left to be done at an uncertain time is frequently left undone,
or at best done but imperfectly.

The first portion of every hour's practice should be devoted to Exercises or Scales.

Practicing a passage, exercise, or scale, does not mean playing it
through once, twice, or thrice, but a careful repetition of it twenty or
thirty times successively; and the practice of the same should be re-
sumed daily till it be executed with correctness and precision, and
with as much fluency as the progress of the pupil will admit.

The degree of rapidity with which anything is played may be conceded to the age or ability of the pupil; but respecting the principle upon which it is played, there must be no compromise. A pupil, therefore, must not conclude anything to be sufficiently practiced until

Not one wrong key is struck.

Not one wrong finger used.

Not one finger down when it ought to be up, or up when it ought to be down.

The hand held in a proper position throughout.

The piece or passage played in proportion, and without looking at the fingers.

Nothing which fails in any of these particulars can be termed correctly done.

RULES TO BE OBSERVED AT PRACTICE.

I.—*Never pass a mistake.*

Whenever a wrong key is struck, a wrong finger used, if a finger be down or up when it ought to be otherwise, or if the passage be not played in proportion, recommence the passage, and continue to do so till it be done correctly. Passing on, intending to rectify the mistake at another time, will only serve to confirm the error, and render it ultimately more difficult to conquer.

II.—*Practice slowly at first.*

Avoiding mistakes is better than having them to rectify. Practice, therefore, slowly at first, and when the passage is done correctly, increase the rapidity to the desired degree. It is certain that that which cannot be done correctly slow will not be correct when done fast. The rapidity may render the incorrectness less observable, but it will not be the less bad.

III.—*Ascertain the nature of the difficulty.*

When any passage is found to be difficult, the first point is to ascertain exactly where, and in *what particular*, the error or the difficulty consists. Suppose, for instance, in a passage of twenty notes, the difficulty lies in the execution of two or three notes only; in that case, practice those two or three notes till they be done with readiness, and then practice the whole passage.

IV.—*Practice with each hand separately.*

It may be sometimes advisable to practice a passage with each hand separately. It may be relied on, that if a passage be not played correctly with one hand at a time, it will not be well done with both hands together.

V.—*Select passages for practice.*

As all parts of a piece will not require the same degree of practice, select those parts in which there is any difficulty, and practice them. Much time is saved by this method. For example, suppose in a page of forty measures there are two which will require practicing fifty times, or more, to do correctly; it is obvious that it will be less trouble, and take less time, to practice the two measures fifty times than the whole page fifty times; besides which, any difficulty will be much sooner surmounted by being played fifty times successively, than if it be played the same number of times, with forty or fifty measures intervening between each repetition.

VI.—*Practice in small portions.*

When a piece contains no decided comparatively difficult passage requiring to be practiced as above, still, it is desirable to practice it in small portions, rather than straight through from the beginning to the end. For instance, suppose two pages containing eighty measures are to be practiced; the pupil will be much more familiarized with the piece by playing portions of eight or sixteen measures, as may be convenient, each twenty times, than if he play the whole eighty measures straight through twenty times.

VII.—*Caution required in selecting passages.*

In selecting passages for practice, it is desirable not to begin or end always at the same place, unless it be a completely detached passage; otherwise a habit of hesitating or stopping at a particular place will be contracted, which may be afterwards difficult to overcome.

VIII.—*Extend and reverse passages.*

It is frequently useful to lengthen or extend a passage to a greater compass than may be required in the piece, or, in fact, to make an exercise of it. For example, if an arpeggio extending two octaves require practice, it will be good policy to practice it to the extent of three or four octaves.

It is also desirable, when the passage will admit of it, to practice both ascending and descending, although only one way may be required in the piece.

IX.—*Repeat correctly six successive times at least.*

No passage that has been badly played should be considered as sufficiently practiced when done once or twice right; SIX SUCCESSIVE times, without error, is the least that can be depended on.

If, on resuming the practice of the same on another occasion, it should be incorrect (as will frequently be the case), it should be practiced till it be done TWELVE SUCCESSIVE times without error, and so on till it can be with certainty played correctly.

X.—*Practice piece as a whole.*

After practicing in detail as above described, the piece must be carefully practiced as a whole from beginning to end. If, in doing this, any mistake should occur, the best remedy is to recommence the whole page or two (nothing fixes the attention so much as this), and continue to do so until

Not one wrong key be struck.

Not one wrong finger used.

Not one finger be down or up when it ought to be otherwise, and until the whole be played through in proportion.

XI.—After correctness, practice for fluency.

Practice, besides being necessary for insuring correctness in any piece or passage, is afterwards requisite for the purpose of gaining more fluency or more finish in the manner of executing it.

XII.—Practice till perfect.

Lastly, it may not be amiss to remark, that although it is desirable, both by diligence and method, to accomplish as much as possible in the shortest time, still, a pupil should remember that, when any piece is played, nobody inquires how often it has been practiced, or how long the performer has been learning it—the only point is, whether it be well or ill done. No stated number of times can, therefore, be fixed upon; but a PIECE SHOULD BE PRACTICED TILL IT BE PERFECT.

POSITION OF THE HAND AND ARM.

The hand and forearm should be in a straight line from the elbow to the middle joint of the second finger, keeping the wrist neither raised nor depressed. The fingers are to be kept moderately bent, and apart (directing particular attention to the second and third fingers, which are more apt to be too close together than the others), so that one finger may be over the centre of each key; and the thumb must always be kept over a key. It is of the highest importance to attend to the keeping of each finger over the centre of a key, for many persons, notwithstanding they may encompass five keys from the thumb to the little finger, by keeping the other fingers at unequal distances, play indistinctly. For example, supposing the right thumb to play C, instead of striking F distinctly with the third finger, they strike both E and F with the third finger. Errors of this sort are not at all uncommon, particularly in arpeggio passages, and should be guarded against from the first, by acquiring a habit of keeping each finger over the centre of a key.

OF THE MANNER OF TOUCHING THE KEYS, OR PUTTING DOWN AND RAISING THE FINGERS.

This is a point not generally sufficiently attended to, but it is one of the greatest importance, and should be thoroughly understood and put in practice at first; for the want of a proper manner of putting down and raising the fingers throws great additional difficulty in the execution of everything that is played, and not only adds difficulty, but gives a bad effect, however perfect the performance may be in all other respects. If the attention be strictly directed to this at first, the proper manner of putting down and raising the fingers will become a *habit*, and will cause no trouble afterwards; whereas, if this be neglected at first, and the pupil be allowed to practice upon a bad or upon no fixed principle, bad habits will be acquired, and become more or less confirmed, in proportion to the degree of practice, and which, if ever they be overcome, must be so at the expense of much labor and time. It is, therefore, essential to prevent any bad habit being contracted.

The rule is simply to hold the finger down on one key till the next is down, but NOT LONGER; or, as it may be otherwise expressed,—

Two keys which are to be played successively must not be held down together, neither must one be raised till the other is down. In order to direct the attention particularly to this point, it may be as well to remark, that if the finger be held down too long after the following key is struck, it may be so in a greater or lesser degree. For instance, suppose C D are to be played successively; C may be held during the whole, or half, or a quarter of the time after D is down, either of which is wrong, though not equally so. It is not unusual with those who have a bad touch, when five successive keys are played, to find the whole five down at once; so that the first is down four times longer than it ought to be, and the others proportionably so.

It may be remarked, that those who hold the fingers down too much in some places generally raise them too soon in others. Raising the finger from one key *before* the next is down must equally, as a general rule, be guarded against, as it gives a broken and disjointed effect.

Let it not, however, be conceived that either holding one key down after the next is struck, or taking one up before the next be down, is wrong, if marked to be so played. What is intended to be impressed on the mind of the pupil is, that the general rule must be to

Hold one key till the next is down, but NOT LONGER.

And no exercise, passage, or lesson should be played in which this cannot be strictly attended to, until a perfect habit of playing upon this principle is acquired; after which the exceptions, such as raising the fingers at the rests, repeated notes, and those marked to be played staccato, etc., must be learned.

OF PRELIMINARY EXERCISES.

It is important, when striking a key with one finger, to do so without moving the others. To acquire the power of doing this, exercises in which some fingers are held firmly down while the others are moving must be practiced. These exercises are termed "preliminary," because they are to be practiced before, and because they differ in principle from all others in this respect, viz., that, for the purpose of acquiring for each finger a free action, independent of the others, those fingers which are not employed in playing are to be held down ; whereas the general rule in all other exercises is, to hold none down but what are actually employed in playing.

The daily practice of these, for a short time previous to other exercises, will always be highly beneficial.

OF LOOKING AT THE FINGERS.

It is essential that the pupil should acquire the power of playing without looking at the fingers. To accomplish this, a little time should occasionally be devoted to this object exclusively.

It must be obvious that the object of all exercises for this purpose will be defeated, if they be played till the pupil remember them ; therefore, the same must never be played twice in one day.

Besides those which are expressly intended (by directing the attention for the time being to that object solely), to teach the pupil to play without looking at the fingers, it must be borne in mind that all the other exercises should be played at first, and afterwards practiced till they can be executed without once looking at the fingers after first placing the hand.

OF THE PRACTICE OF EXERCISES.

The greatest difficulties arise from a want of attention to the position of the hand, and the manner of putting down as well as taking up the fingers at the proper places. The attention of the pupil must, therefore, be directed to these points in the practice of exercises until it becomes habitual both to hold the hands well and touch the keys in a proper manner. Exercises are classed for different purposes, such as the practice of single notes, double notes, arpeggios, etc., etc., and, as passages similar to all exercises will be found in lessons, they will, after being practiced and mastered as exercises, not appear as difficulties when they occur.

ORDER OF LEARNING AND PRACTICING THE SCALES.

When the pupil is sufficiently advanced, the Scales should be learned and practiced daily.

On Mondays, or any fixed day of the week, learn one Major Scale, taken in regular order, and its relative Minor, and practice the same six times, or more, every day during the week; but if, at the week's end, they are not done correctly, and with as much fluency as may be desired, the same must be practiced for a week, or as many weeks more as may be requisite, before proceeding to the next.

The Scales should be practiced in several different ways.

First mode of going through the Scales.

Practice with each hand separately, ascending and descending six or more times without intermission.

It may not be useless to remark that, in whichever mode they be practiced, the following points must be attended to:

The hand must be held in a proper position throughout.

As one finger goes down, the former must be raised, so that always one, and only one, key be down at a time.

In passing the thumb under the fingers, or fingers over the thumb, great care must be taken to do so with as little motion of the hand as possible.

When this is thoroughly, though perhaps slowly, accomplished, the pupil may proceed upon the same principle to the Scale next in succession, until all have been gone through with.

When all the Scales have been practiced through in this manner, it will, most probably, be desirable to recommence, and go through the same course again, before proceeding to the next mode.

Second mode of going through the Scales.

Practice with both hands together, ascending and descending eight or more times successively. The same directions as to position of the hand, correctness, and repetition, if necessary, of the same Scales, must be attended to in this and succeeding modes, as are recommended in the first mode of practicing the Scales; also, the repetition of the whole course, if necessary.

Third mode of going through the Scales.

Instead of ascending and descending as before, practice each Scale six or more times, ascending only, and then as many times descending only, with each hand separately.

Practice progressively with increased rapidity.

Fourth mode of going through the Scales.

Practice each Scale eight times, or more, ascending only, and then as many times descending only, with both hands together.

Practice progressively with increased rapidity.

Fifth mode of going through the Scales.

Practice each Scale in thirds eight times, or more.

To play a Scale in thirds, begin with the *right hand* on the *third* of the scale, with the finger that would have been upon it had the scale been commenced on the key tone, playing at the same time with the left hand in the usual manner.

Sixth mode of going through the Scales.

Practice each Scale in sixths eight times, or more.

To play a scale in sixths, begin with the *left hand* on the *third* of the scale (viz., a sixth below the right hand), with the finger that would have been upon it had the scale been commenced with the key tone, playing at the same time with the right hand in the usual manner.

ON THE PRACTICE OF OLD LESSONS.

It is desirable to keep up the practice of the old lessons, but it is presumed that a little time will suffice for that purpose, if they have been properly learned; therefore, at the SECOND HOUR'S PRACTICE, on Tuesdays, Thursdays, and Saturdays, practice an old lesson; if it be done properly, proceed to another; but if not, resume the practice of the same on the appointed days, till it be perfect.

CHAPTER XXXII.

PRONOUNCING DICTIONARY OF MUSICAL TERMS.

In the preparation of this Dictionary we have not aimed at completeness; we have merely tried to furnish a list of such technical words and
phrases as the piano and organ pupil will most frequently need.

Note.—As most of the words in this vocabulary are from the Italian language, it becomes necessary to explain a few peculiarities which form an important feature in the
pronunciation of that language—viz., *c* sounds like *k*, as *capo* (kapo), except before *e*
and *i*, when it is like *ch* in *chat*, as *vivace* (vē-vä'-tchē), *velocita* (vä-lō-tchē-tä') ; *g* as in *go*
(*gavŏt*), except before *e* and *i*, as *giusto* (joos'-to), *leggere* (lej-jä'-rē) ; *s* between two
vowels sounds like *z*, as *amoroso* (äm-ō-rō'-zō), otherwise like English *s ; z* sounds like
ts in *flits*, as *mezzo* (mät'-so) ; French *n* has the sound of *n* in *bank*.

A, (It. äh.) The name of a pitch ; *It.*
prep. to, by, at, in, with.

Ab, (It. prep. ähb.) From, of.

Abbandono, (It. ä-bän-dō'-nō,) **Con.**
With abandon.

Abbreviations.

Accel., accelerando.	*Dim.*, diminuendo.
Accom., accompani-	*Dol.*, dolce.
ment.	*Esprv.*, espressivo.
Adgo., or *Ado.*, ada-	*F.*, forte.
gio.	*F. F.*, fortissimo.
Ad. lib., ad libitum.	*F. P.*, forte-piano.
Affet., affettuoso.	*Fz., Fs.*, forzando ;
All' ot., all' ottavio.	sforzando.
Allo., allegro.	*G.*, gauche.
Allgtto., allegretto.	*L. H.*, left hand.
Andno., andantino.	*Leg.*, legato.
Andte., andante.	*Len.*, lentando.
Arc., arco.	*Lo., luo.*, loco or
Arpio., arpeggio.	luogo.
A. T., a tempo.	*Marc.*, marcato.
Coll' 8va, coll' ot-	*M. D.*, mano destra ;
tava.	main droite.
C. D., colla destra.	*Mez.*, mezzo.
C. S., colla sinistra.	*M. V.*, mezzo voce.
Cad., cadenza.	*P.*, piano.
Cal., callandro.	*Ped.*, pedale.
Cho., chorus.	*P. F.*, piu forte.
Clar., clarinetto.	*Pizz.*, pizzicato.
Claro., clarino.	*P. P.*, pianissimo ;
Cresc., crescendo.	piu piano.
D., destra ; droite.	*R. H.*, right hand.
D. C., da capo.	*Rall.*, rallentando.
D. S., dal segno.	*Rf., Rfs.* rinfor-
Decres., decrescen-	zando.
do.	*Rit.*, ritardando

Riten., ritenuto.	*String.*, stringendo.
S., or *sin.*, sinistra.	*Sym.*, symphony.
Scherz., scherzando.	*T.*, tasto ; tutti ; tem-
Seg., segue.	*Ten.*, tenuto. [po.
Sem., sempre.	*Tr.*, trillo.
Sfz., sforzando.	*Trem.*, tremolando.
Smorz., smorzando.	*T. S.*, taslo solo.
Sost., sostenuto.	*U. C.*, una corda.
S. S., senza Sordini.	*Unis.*, unison.
S. T., senza Tempo.	*Var.*, variazione.
Stacc., staccato.	*V. S.*, volti subito.

(The above list contains all the abbreviations which are in common use. For the
definitions and pronunciations of the words,
see under the words themselves throughout
the Dictionary.)

A capella, (It. ä cä-pĕl'-lä.) In church
style—*i. e.*, the voices without accompaniment.

A capricio, (It. ä cä-prē'-tchō.) At
caprice ; at pleasure.

Accelerando, (It. ä-tchel-ä-rōn'-dō.)
Accelerating the time.

Accentuato (It. ä-tchen-too-ä'-tō.) Accented.

Acciaccatura, (It. at-tchack-a-too'-
rä,) from *acciacare*, to crush. A short *appoggiatura* (*q.v.*)which is crushed against
the principal note, as it were (*i. e.*, both
struck at the same instant), but which is
instantly released and the principal key
held ; of great service in organ music in
giving the effect of an accent, or sforzando, to either single tones or chords.

Accompagnamento, (It. ä-kōm-
pan-yä-män'-to.) Accompaniment.

āte, äh, ạll, ăt, ạway ; ēke, ĕnd ; īre, ĭt, bịrd ; ōde, ŏn, ōr, wọrd ; ōōze ; lūte, hŭt,
bụrn ; ü French sound.

185

Adagio, (It. ä-dä'-jo.) Slow; a slow movement.

Adagissimo, (It. ä-dä-jees'-I-mo.) Superlative degree of adagio.

Ad libitum, (Lat. ad lĭb'-I-tum.) At pleasure.

A dur, (G. ä dōōr.) Key of A major.

Affettuoso, (It. ä-fĕt-oo-ō'-zō.) Affectionately, tenderly. **Con Affettuoso,** with feeling.

Agilita, (It. ä-jĭl'-I-tä.) Agility, sprightliness, quickness.

Agitato, (It. äj-I-tä'-tō.) Agitated, restless; usually implies hurrying.

Al, All, Alla, (It. äl, äl'-lä.) To the; in the style of.

Alla Breve, (It.) $\frac{2}{2}$ measure, usually marked C.

Allegretto, (It. äl-le-grä'-to.) A little quick; not so quick as allegro.

Allegro, (It. äl-läy'-grō.) Cheerful, joyful; a time mark indicating a quick movement.

Al segno, (It. sän'-yō). From the sign; return to the sign and proceed to the word *Fine*. See *Dal Segno*.

Alt. (It. ält.) High; as, *A in alt*, the A represented by the first added line above of treble staff.

Alta, or **8va,** (It. äl'-tä, or at-tä'-vä.) An octave higher than written.

Amabile, (It. a-mä'-bĕ-lä.) Lovingly; gentle; tender.

A moll, (Ger. ä mŏlf.) Key of A minor.

Amoroso, (It. ăm-ō-rō'-zō.) In a loving style; with warmth.

Andante, (It. ăn-dän'-tä.) Literally, going at a moderate pace; the name of a moderate movement.

Andantino, (It. ăn-dan-tee'-no.) Diminutive of *Andante*; and, as *Andante* means, literally "*going*," its diminutive must mean "going a little," "rather going"—*i. e.*, not going quite so fast—and consequently indicates a slower movement than *Andante*. Andantino is, unfortunately, defined in two opposite ways—by some as faster than *Andante*, by others as slower, resulting from the ambiguity of its literal meaning—viz., "rather going." Most modern lexicographers, including Grove, Stainer and Barrett, define it as "slower than *Andante*." Webster and Worcester both agree in defining it "less slow than *Andante*." As a proof of the uncertainty with which this term is used, turn to the oratorio of "Elijah." The three movements—viz., "If with all your hearts," marked *Andante con moto;* "The Lord hath exalted thee," marked *Andante;* and "Oh rest in the Lord," marked *An-*

dantino—are all performed in the same time—viz., $\frac{1}{2} = 72$.

Anima, (It. an'-ĕ-mä.) Life. **Con anima,** with animation.

A piacere, (It. ä 'pē-ä-tchä'-rĕ.) At pleasure; however, *rallentando* (*q. v.*) is usually implied.

Appassionata, (It. ä-päs-sĕ-ō-nä'-tä.) Impassioned. Applied by Cranz, the publisher, to Beethoven's sonata op. 57.

Appoggiatura, (It. ăp-pŏdg-jä-too'-rä,) from *appoggiare,* "to lean upon" (Ger. *Vorschlag, Vorhalt;* Fr. *Port de Voix*). A melodic ornament, both vocal and instrumental. It consists in suspending or delaying a tone by means of a tone introduced before it, its time, whether long or short, being always taken from the value of the principal tone. The *long A.* receives half the time of the following note, and is expressed by a grace note; the *short A.* is crushed against the following tone, and is expressed by a grace note with an oblique dash through the stem. The *short A.* is synonymous with *acciaccatura* (*q. v.*).

Appoggiatura, Double, consists of two short notes before a note of melody, one below and the other above the principal note. The first may be at any distance from the principal note, but the second should be only one degree removed. They have no fixed duration, but are generally slower when applied to a long note. In all cases the time of both is taken from the principal note.

Ardito, (It. är-de'-tō.) Ardor; warmth.

Aria, Italian for air or melody (är'-iä.) **Arietta,** a little air.

Arpeggio, (It. är-pădg'-jŏ,) from *arpa,* the harp. The tones of a chord performed in succession instead of simultaneously. A broken chord.

As, (Ger. äs.) A flat (A♭).

Assai, (It. äs-sä'-ĕ.) Very—*e. g.,* *allegro assai*, very fast.

A tempo, (It. ä tĕm'-pō.) In time; a term denoting a return to the original time after a change has been made. More correctly written *a tempo primo,* in the time of the first movement.

A tre, (It. ä trä'.) For three.

A tre mano, (It. ä trä mä'-nō). For three (Fr. *a tre mains*).

Attacca, (It. ät-täk'-kä.) Attack; as, *attacca subito*, attack the next quickly.

Atto, (It. ät'-tō.) Act.

B, seventh tone in the key of C; Ger. H (häh); in German the name B indicates the key of B flat.

Baritono clef. The bass clef applied to the third line.

Bass clef. The sign of the bass staff.

It fixes *middle C* on the first added line above.

Basso continuo, (It. bäs'-so kŏn-tē-noo'-ŏ.) Synonymous with *thorough bass* (*q. v.*).

B dur, (Ger. bay dōōr.) B major.

Bellezza, (It. bel-lät'-sä.) Beauty of tone or expression.

Ben, Bene, (It. bān, bā-nĕ.) Well, good.

Bis, (It. bēse.) Twice.

Breve. A double whole note; only used in church music.

Brilliante, (It. and Fr. brĭl-yän'-tä.) Brilliantly.

Brio, (It. brē'-ŏ.) Spirit, vigor, force.

C. The name of a pitch; key-tone or tonic of the Ionic scale of the church modes; the sign of quadruple measure.

Cadenza, (It. kä-dĕn'-tsä.) A more or less elaborate flourish of indefinite form, introduced immediately preceding the entire close, or of an important section of the composition. In instrumental music cadenzas are sometimes continued through several pages.

Calando, (It. kăl-län'-dŏ.) With decreasing force.

Cantabile, (It. kăn-tä'-bĕ-lä,) from *cantare,* to sing. In a graceful singing style.

Capo, (It. kă'-pŏ.) Head or commencement.

Capriccio, (It. kă-prē'-tchŏ.) A freak, whim, or fancy. A composition irregular in form.

Capriccioso, (It. kă-prē-tchē-ŏ'-zo.) Capriciously.

Choir Organ. The part of the organ containing most of the solo stops.

Chorale, (kŏ-räl.) A slow sacred tune.

Chromatic. Literally *colored.* The tones intermediate between the diatonic tones of a key.

Chromatic Scale. A scale in which all the tones, intermediate and diatonic, occur in successive order.

Clef, (Fr. klĕf.) Literally a key. A character used at the beginning of a staff to determine the pitches.

Coda, (It. kŏ'-dä.) A phrase added to a composition as a conclusion.

Commodo, (It. kŏm-mŏ'-do.) Easily, at will, without haste.

Con, (It. kŏwn.) With; as, *con brio,* with spirit.

Con Delicattezza, (It. del-lĕ-cä-tĕt'-sä.) With delicacy.

Con Disperazione, (It. dĕs-pär-rät-sĕ-ŏ'-nĕ.) With desperation.

Con Dolore, (It. dŏ-lŏr'-rĕ.) With sadness.

Con Eleganza, (It. el-ā-gänt'-sä.) With elegance.

Con Energico, (It. ĕn-er-gee'-cŏ.) With energy.

Con Espressione, (It. es-pres-sĭ-ŏn'-nĕ.) With expression.

Con Fuoco, (It. foo-ąw'-cŏ.) With fire.

Con Furia, (It. foo'-ri-ä.) With fury.

Con Grazia, (It. grät'-si-ä.) With grace.

Con Impeto, (It. ĭm-pät'-tŏ). With impetuosity.

Con Justo, (It. joos'-tŏ.) With exactness.

Con Moto. With steady motion.

Con Precisione, (It. prā-tchē-zĕ-ŏ'-nĕ.) With precision.

Con Sordini, (It. kŏwn sôr-dee'-nee.) With mutes.

Con Spirito, (It. spĕr'-ē-tŏ.) With spirit.

Contralto, (It. kŏn-träl'-tŏ.) The lowest female voice. The usual compass is from G or F♯ below to C or D above.

Con Variazione, (It. vä-rē-ät-sĕ-ŏ'-nĕ.) With variations.

Con Velocita, (It. vä-lŏ-tchē-tä'.) With velocity.

Corda, (It.) String or cord; as, *una corda,* with one string—*i. e.,* with soft pedal.

Corona, (It. kŏr-rŏ'-nä.) The Hold (⌒).

Crescendo, (It. krĕs-shän'dŏ.) With increasing power.

Da, (It. dä.) From; also compounded with *lo;* as, *dal, dallo,* from the.

Da capo, (It. dä käp'-o.) From the beginning.

Da capo al Fine, (It. äl fee'-nay.) From the beginning to the word *Fine,* or end.

Dal segno, (It. däl sän'-yo.) From the sign.

Damper Pedal. Improperly called "loud pedal." A mechanism which raises all the dampers at once, thus allowing the strings to continue to vibrate.

Dampers. Cushions of felt resting on the strings of the piano forte to prevent vibration.

Decrescendo, (It. dä'-crä-shän'-dŏ.) A gradual decrease of power.

Diminuendo, (It. dĭm-in-oo-ĕn'-dŏ.) Diminishing in power; *decrescendo* (*q. v.*).

Dolce, (It. dŏl-tchay.) Sweetly; also tne name of a soft, string-toned organ stop.

Dolcissimo, (It. dŏl-tchē'-sĭ-mŏ.) Superlative of *dolce.*

Doloroso, (It. dŏ-lŏ-rŏ'-zŏ.) Grievingly.

Dominant. Literally ruler; five of the key.

āte, äh, ạll, ăt, ạway; ĕke, ĕnd; ĭre, ĭt, bįrd; ŏde, ŏn, ŏr, wọrd; ōōze; lūte, hŭt, bụrn; ü French sound.

Doppel Flote, (Ger. döp-pel flō-tå.) An organ stop composed of wooden stopped pipes with two mouths.

Doppio, (It.) Double; as, *doppio movemento,* doubly as fast or twice as fast; *doppio pedale,* with double pedals.

Dot. A point placed after a note or rest which adds one half to the rhythmical value of the note or rest; a second dot adds half as much as the first.

Double Bar. A broad bar drawn across the staff to indicate the ending and beginning of the music which is applied to a line of words; in instrumental music it denotes the end of a strain.

Double Flat. Two flats before a note, indicating that a tone two half-steps below is to be used—*e. g.,* if in the key of D flat major flat 6 were wanted, it would be expressed by B double flat (B♭♭), and would be produced on the piano or organ by pressing the *A key.*

Doublets. Two equal tones performed in the time of one pulse.

Droite, (Fr. drwåt.) Right; as, *main droite* (mång drwåt), right hand.

Dur, (Ger. dōōr.) Literally hard. German name for major mode.

Dynamics. That department of musical science which relates to, or treats of, the force of musical sounds. The dynamic degrees range from *pp,* which is the softest possible, through *p. m.* and *f.* to *ff.,* which is the loudest possible.

E dur, (Ger.) The key of E major.

E moll, (Ger.) The key of E minor.

Energico, (It. en-ĕr-gĕĕ'-co.) Energetic.

Es (Ger. ås.) E flat. *Es moll,* E flat minor.

Etude, (Fr. å'-tood.) A study, in contradistinction to an exercise.

Extravaganza, (It. gänt'-så.) A caricature.

Fantasia, (It. fån-tä'-zëä.) A fantasy.

Figured Bass. A bass with figures which indicate the accompanying harmony; *thorough bass (q. v.).*

Finale, (It. fĕ-nä'-lĕ.) ⎫
Fine, (It. fee'nĕ.) ⎭ The end.

Form. The shape or structure of a composition; the arrangement of musical ideas into phrases, sections, periods, etc.

Forte, (It. fŏr'-tĕ.) Loud; the fourth degree of power.

Fortissimo, (It. fŏr-tees'-ĕ-mŏ.) As loud as possible; the fifth degree of power.

Forzando, (It. fort-sän'-dŏ.) Sudden force.

Fugue, (fūg.) A composition in contrapuntal style, in which a subject, taken by one part or voice, is answered by other voices according to certain rules.

Fuoco, (It. foo-g'-kŏ.) Fire, energy.

Furioso, (It. foo-rĕ-ŏ'-zŏ.) Furiously.

Gavotte, Gavote, or **Gavot,** (Fr. gå-vŏt'.) It. *gavotta.* Derived from the *Gavoto,* a people inhabiting a mountainous district in France called *Gap;* a brisk kind of dance or tune, the air of which has two lively strains, each of which is repeated. The dance was difficult and complicated, hence it became more popular as an instrumental piece.

Giocoso, (It. jŏ-kŏ'-zo.) Jocosely.

Giusto, (It. joos'-tŏ.) Exact; as, *tempo giusto,* in exact time.

Glissando, (It. glis-sän'-dŏ.) Playing a rapid passage on the piano by sliding the tips of the fingers along on the keys; a rapid slur in violin playing.

Grandioso, (It. grän-dĕ-ŏ'-zŏ.) Grandly.

Grave, (It. grä'-vä.)   slow; solemn.

Gravita, (It. grä-vĕ-tä'.) Gravity; majesty.

Grazia, (It. grät'-se-ä.) Grace; elegance.

Grazioso, (It. grät-se-ŏ'-zo.) Gracefully.

Gruppetto, (It. groo-pĕt'-to.) Literally, a little group; a turn.

Gusto, (It. goos'-to.) Taste; as, *con gusto,* with taste.

Gustoso, (It. goos-tŏ'-zo.) Same as above.

H, (hä.) The German name for B. What they call B (bäy) is our B flat.

Half-Step. A term of measurement, being the smallest now in use; it is equal to an augmented prime and a minor second.

H dur, (Ger. hä dōōr.) The key of B major.

Impeto, Impetuoso, (It. ĕm-pä'-tŏ, ĕm-pä-too-ŏ'-zo.) Impetuously.

In Alt. Tones above the fifth line treble staff.

Indeciso, (It. ĕn-dä-tchĕ'-zo.) Indecision; unsteady.

In Tempo, (It. ĕn tĕm'-pŏ.) In time.

Interval. The difference of pitch between two tones; also their effect when produced simultaneously.

Introduction. A short preparatory movement.

Introit, (Fr. äng-trwä.) Entrance; a hymn or anthem sung or chanted while the priest enters within the rails of the altar; now used as a name of any vocal composition appropriate to the opening of church service.

Inversion. Literally the act of turning over or backward. In music it has five significations—viz.: I. In counterpoint it signifies the repetition of a phrase or passage with several intervals. II. In double counterpoint it indicates that the upper part is placed below the lower, or *vice versa*. III. Intervals are said to be inverted when the lower tone is so changed as to become the higher. IV. A chord is inverted when any tone other than its fundamental is taken in the lowest part. V. Pedal point (*organ point*) is said to be inverted when the sustained tone is transferred from the bass to an upper part.

Key. A family of tones.

Key-tone. The tonic ; the tone from which all other tones are reckoned.

Knee-stop. An organ-stop worked by the knee.

Largo. Slow.

Leading-tone. Seven of any key; minor second below the tonic.

Legatissimo, (It. lä-gä-tēs'-ĕ-mō.) Superlative of legato.

Legato, (It. lä-gä'-tō.) Connected ; each tone of a phrase being continued until the next is heard.

Leit-motif, (Ger. līt'-mo-teef.) The guiding theme.

Lentando, (It. lĕn-tän'-dō.) Slackening the time. Same as *rallentando (q. v.).*

Lento, (It. län'-tō.) Slow.

Loco. As written ; used after 8va.

M. *Mezzo (q. v.), metronome (q. v.), mano (q. v.).*

Ma, (It. mä.) But.

Main, (Fr. mäng.) The hand.

Mano, (It. mä'-no.) The hand.

Mediant. The third above the tonic. Three of the key.

Meno, (It. mä'-nō.) Less.

Metronome, (mĕt'-rō-nōm.) An instrument for measuring time. A clockwork, to the pendulum of which is attached a sliding ball. The frequency of the pulsations is ascertained by placing the top of the ball opposite the figures on the graduated scale—*e. g.,* if the top of the ball be placed at 60, the metronome will give 60 ticks to the minute.

Mezzo, (It. mät'-sō.) Half, medium.

Moll, (Ger. mōl.) Soft ; minor.

Molto, (It. mōl'-tō.) Much ; very much.

Morceau, (Fr. môr-sō'.) Short musical piece.

Morendo, (It. mō-rän'-dō.) Dying away; is rarely used except in slow movements, and usually indicates diminuendo and rallentando combined.

Mosso, (It. mō'-sō.) Motion ; as, *meno mosso,* less motion.

Moto, (It. mō'-tō.) Movement.

Natural. A character used to cancel the effect of a previous flat or sharp. Hence *cancel* is rapidly supplanting *natural* as the name of the character.

Nocturne, (Fr.) A night-piece or serenade.

Non, (It. nôn.) Not.

O, (It. ō.) Or.

Obligato, (It. ōb-lē-gä'-tō.) Literally bound ; obligatory, must not be omitted.

Octave. Eight degrees or tones from any given tone, either above or below.

Octet. For eight voices or instruments.

Pedal. Pertaining to the foot ; hence, a lever operated by the foot.

Pensoso, (It. pĕn-sō'-zō.) Pensively.

Pesante, (It. pä-zän'-tĕ.) Ponderous, heavy.

Phrase. A short tone-chain which makes sense, but not complete sense.

Piacere, (It. pē-ä-tchä'-rĕ.) Pleasure, fancy.

Piano, (It. pē-ä'-nō.) Soft ; gentle.

Piu, (It. pē'-oo.) More.

Pizzicato, (It. pĕt-sē-kä'-tō.) Literally *pinched ;* the strings of the orchestra snapped with the fingers.

Placido, (It. plä-tchĕ'-do.) Placid ; pleasant.

Plagal. Literally sidewise, slanting. Old church modes in which the melody was confined between the dominant and its octave.

Plagal Cadence. A cadence in which the final tonic chord is preceded by the sub-dominant.

Poco, (It. pō'-kō.) Little.

Polacca, (It. pō-lä'-kä.) A Polish dance in 3-4 measure.

Polka. A Polish dance in 2-4 measure, the third 8th-note being accented.

Polonaise, (pōl-ō-nāz'.) A movement of three quarter-notes in a measure, with the rhythmical cæsura on the last ; also a dance adapted to such music ; a *polacca (q. v.).*

Portamento, (It. pōr-tä-mān'-to.) A carrying of the voice, or gliding from one tone to another.

Postludium, (It. pōst-loo'-dē-ŭm.) A concluding voluntary.

Potpourri, (Fr. pō-poor-ee'.) Literally a mixture ; a piece of music made up of different airs strung together ; a medley.

Precipitato, (It. prä-tchē-pē-tä'-tō.) In a precipitate manner ; hurriedly.

Precisione, (It. prä-tchē-zē-ō-nĕ.) Precision ; exactness.

Prelude, (It. prä'-lood.) A short introductory piece.

Presto, (It. präs'-tō.) Quickly.

Prima, (It. prĕ'-mä.) First.

Prima Vista, (It. vēs'-tä.) At first sight.

Prima Volta, (It. vōl'-tä.) The first time.

āte, äh, all, ăt, away; ēke, ĕnd ; īre, ĭt, bĭrd ; ōde, ŏn, ôr, wŏrd ; ōōze ; lūte, hŭt, bŭrn ; ü French sound.

Program. An order of exercises.

Quadrulets. Four equal tones performed in the time of one pulse.

Questa, (It. quās'-tä.) This; that.

Quintolets. Five equal tones performed in the time of one pulse.

Rallentando, (It. räl-ĕn-tän'-dŏ.) Gradually slower and softer.

Recitativo, (It. rä-tchĕ-tä-tee'-vŏ.) A musical declamation.

Redowa, (rĕd'-ŏ-wä.) A Bohemian dance in 2-4 and 3-4 measure, alternately.

Refrain. The chorus of a song; that which is repeated at the end of each stanza; a ritornello (*q. v.*).

Religioso, (It. rĕ-lĕ-jĕ-ŏ'-zŏ.) Religiously; devoutly.

Retard. Gradually slower.

R. H. Right hand.

Rinforzando, (It. rĕn-fŏrt-sän'-dŏ.) Reinforcing; strengthening—*i. e.*, becoming stronger and stronger.

Ritardando, (It. rĕt-är-dän'-dŏ.) Delaying the time gradually.

Ritenuto, (It. rĕ-tĕn-oo'-tŏ.) Kept back; detained. Differs from *ritardando* in that it is done at once, instead of being done gradually.

Ritornello (It. rĭt-ŏr-nāl'-lŏ.) An interlude; a short period following each stanza, often consisting of the *burden of the song.*

Romanza, (It. rŏ-mänt'-sä.) Literally romance. A short lyric tale set to music; a song or short instrumental piece in ballad style.

Rondo. A round. A composition in which the first strain is repeated at the end of each of the other strains.

Rubato, (It. roo-bä'-tŏ.) Literally robbed, stolen; as, *tempo rubato,* borrowed time—*i. e.*, some tones held longer than written, while others are proportionately curtailed.

Scena, (It. shä'-nä.) A scene or portion of an opera.

Scherzando, (It. skĕrt-sän-dŏ.) Playfully.

Scherzo, (It. skĕrt'-sŏ.) Play; sport.

Scordato, (It. skŏr-dä'-tŏ.) Out of tune; false.

Sempre, (It. sĕm'-prä.) Always.

Senza, (It. sĕnt'-sä.) From the Lat. *sine,* without; as, *senza organo,* without organ.

Septolets. Seven equal tones performed in the time of one pulse.

Sextolets. Six equal tones performed in the time of one pulse.

Sforza, (It. sfŏrt'-sä.) Forcing or forced.

Sforzando, (It. sfŏrt-sän'-do.) See above.

Si-bemol, (Fr. sĕ-bĕ-mol'.) B flat.

Signature. Sharps or flats placed at the beginning of a piece to indicate the key.

Sinistra, (It. sĭn'-ĭs-trä.) The left hand.

Slur. A curved line connecting two or more notes, to show that they are to be sung to one syllable or played *legato.*

Smorzando, (It. smŏrt-sän'-do.) Literally quenched; extinguished; growing gradually fainter and softer; dying away.

Sonata, (It. sŏ-nä'-tä.) An extended composition, usually consisting of three or four movements.

Soprano, (It. sŏ-prä'-nŏ.) The highest female voice.

Sordino, (It. sŏr-dĕ'-nŏ.) A mute.

Sostenuto, (It. sŏs-tĕn-oo'-tŏ.) Sustaining the tone.

Sotto Voce, (It. sŏ-tŏ vŏ-tchĕ.) Under the voice—*i. e.*, in a very soft voice.

Spiritoso, (It. spĕr-rĕ-tŏ'-zŏ.) In a spirited manner.

Staccato, (It. stä-kä'-tŏ.) Literally detached; distinct; separated.

Stretto, (It. strä-tŏ'.) Literally close, pressed. That part of a fugue in which the subject and its answer are brought closely together.

Stringendo, (It, strĭn-jän'-dŏ.) Literally to urge, to press; hastening the time.

Sub-bass, (sŭb-băse'.) Low bass; the 16-feet pedal stop of an organ.

Subdominant. Four of the key.

Subito, (It. soo-bĕ'-tŏ.) Quickly.

Submediant. Six of the key.

Subtonic. Seven of the key; the leading-tone.

Suite, (Fr. sweet.) A form consisting of several movements, usually five, out of which grew the sonata (*q. v.*).

Supertonic. Two of the key.

Suspension. The withholding of one or more tones proper to a chord while retaining a tone or tones of the preceding chord, thus producing a momentary dissonance.

Symphony. The most important of all instrumental forms; a *sonata* for full orchestra.

Syncopation, from the Lat. *syncope* (sĭn'-ko-pee), to strike, to cut off. The displacement of the usual accent, either by cutting it away from the commonly accented pulse, and driving it over to that part of a measure not usually accented, or by prolonging a tone begun in a weak pulse past the instant when the usual accent should occur.

Tace, (It. tä'-tchä.) Same as *tacet (q. v.).*

Tacet, (Lat tä'-set.) It is silent; a direction for a vocal or instrumental part to be silent.

Tarantella, (It. tär-än-tál'-lä.) A peculiar Italian dance in 6-8 measure ; named after the spider called *tarantula*, whose bite is popularly supposed to be cured by music.

Tasto Solo. Without harmony ; all parts in unison.

Tempo. Time ; movement.

Tenor. The highest male voice.

Tenor Robusto, (It. rō-boos'-tō.) A strong tenor voice.

Tenuto, (It. těn-noo'-tō.) Sustained ; held.

Terzetto, (It. tārt-sāt'-tō.) A short piece for three voices.

Thema, (It. tä'-mä,) **Theme,** (Fr. tăm.) Theme. A simple tune on which variations are made ; the principal melodic subject.

Thorough Bass. A species of musical shorthand, invented by Ludovico Viadani early in the seventeenth century. It consists of the bass part, with figures added which indicate the accompanying harmonies.

Tierce, (Fr. těrs.) A third.

Tierce de Picardie. The major third used in the final chord of a minor composition. So called from having been first used in the province of Picardy.

Tonic. The key-tone ; the tone from which all other tones are reckoned.

Tre corda, (It. trä kôr'-dä.) Literally three strings ; discontinue the soft pedal.

Tremando, (It. trä-män'-dō.) Trembling ; vibrating.

Tremolo, (It. trä'-mō-lō.) A note or chord made to quiver or shake.

Tremulant. The name of an organ-stop which causes the tones to tremble.

Triad. A chord consisting of three tones —viz., a fundamental with its third and its fifth.

Trill. A rapid alternation of two contiguous tones of the key ; a shake.

Triplets. Three equal tones performed in the time of one pulse.

Tromba, (It. tròm'-bä.) Trumpet ; a reed-stop in the organ.

Tuba, (It. too'-bä.) Bass trumpet ; a powerful reed-stop in the organ.

Turn, a *grupetto* (*q. v.*).

Tutti in forza, (It. toot'-tä lä fōrt'-sä.) With all force ; as loud as possible.

Tutte corde, (It. toot-tä kôr-dä.) All the strings ; discontinue the soft pedal.

Tutti, (It. too'-tē.) All ; used after solo passages to indicate that all are to join in the performance.

Un, Una, (It. oon, oon'-ä.) A ; one.

Una corda, (It. oo'-nä kôr-dä.) Literally one string ; a direction to use the soft pedal.

Veloce, (It. vě-lō'-tchä.) Rapidly.

Velocissimo, (It. vě-lō-tchēē'-sēē-mo.) Very rapidly.

Vibrato, (It. vě-brä'-tō.) A tremulous quality of tone.

Viola, (It. vē-ŏ lä.) See under *Violoncello.*

Violin. See under *Violoncello.*

Violoncello, (It. vē-ō-lŏn-tchäl'-lō.) Literally, the little *violono*. The string family may be classified as follows :

1. Violin............ Treble.
2. Viola............. Tenor.
3. Violoncello ....Bass.
4. Violone..........Double Bass.

These form the *quartet of strings*, and if a 2d violin is added, they are still called the *quartet of strings*.

Violono, (It. vē-ō-lō'-nō,) or **Violone.** See under *Violoncello.*

Virtuoso, (It. vēr-too-ō'-zō.) A skillful performer upon a special instrument.

Vivace, (It. vē-vä'-tchä.) Quickly ; sprightly.

Voce, (It. vō'-tchä.) The voice.

Voce di Petto, (It. vō'-tchä dē pět'-tō.) Chest voice.

Voce di Testa, (It. vō'-tchä dě těs'-tä.) Head voice.

Volti Subito, (It. vŏl'-tē soo-bēē'-tō.) Turn quickly.

Vox, (Lat. vŏx.) The voice.

Vox Angelica, (Lat. vŏx än-gěl'-ĭ-cä.) Angel voice. An organ stop of 8-feet tone.

Vox Celeste, (vŏx sä-lěst',) or **Voix Celeste** (vwä.) Celestial voice. An organ-stop producing a wavy effect.

Vox Humana, (Lat. vŏx hoo-män'-nä.) Literally the human voice. An organ reed-stop made to imitate the human voice.

āte, äh, all, ăt, away ; ēke, ĕnd ; ir , ĭt, bĭrd ; ōde, ŏn, or, wŏre ; ōoze ; lūte. nŭt, bŭrn! r, F ẽach sound.

INDEX BY CHAPTERS.

J. M. ARMSTRONG & CO.,
MUSIC TYPOGRAPHERS AND ELECTROTYPERS,
710 SANSOM ST., PHILADELPHIA.

www.ingramcontent.com/pod-product-compliance
Lightning Source LLC
Chambersburg PA
CBHW030840270326
41928CB00007B/1143